THE AUTHOR

Ralph A. Wooster is professor and head of the Department of History at Lamar State College of Technology, Beaumont, Texas. A graduate of the University of Texas, Professor Wooster is past president of the East Texas Historical Association and the Texas Association of College Teachers and is a member of the Board of Directors and a fellow of the Texas State Historical Association. He has contributed more than thirty articles to professional historical journals and is author of *The Secession Conventions of the South* (1962).

THE PEOPLE IN POWER

# THE PEOPLE
☆☆☆☆☆☆☆☆☆☆☆☆☆☆☆☆☆☆☆☆☆☆☆☆☆☆☆☆☆☆☆☆☆☆☆
# IN POWER

*Courthouse and Statehouse*
*in the Lower South*
*1850–1860*

RALPH A. WOOSTER

THE UNIVERSITY OF TENNESSEE PRESS
KNOXVILLE

LIBRARY OF CONGRESS CATALOG CARD NUMBER 69–20116
STANDARD BOOK NUMBER 87049–090–7


*First edition.*

IN MEMORY OF SAM EVANS

FRIEND AND COLLEAGUE

# PREFACE

Several years ago when studying the secession movement of 1860–61, I was impressed by the fact that comparatively little had been written about the structure of southern state and county government for the late antebellum period. While both Charles S. Sydnor in his *Development of Southern Sectionalism, 1819–1848,* and Fletcher M. Green in his *Constitutional Development in the South Atlantic States, 1776–1860,* dealt with this theme in part and while there were a number of studies of political developments within individual states, I could find no work devoted completely to southern state and county government before secession. Nowhere was there in a single volume an examination of what the various state and county offices were on the eve of the Civil War, how they evolved, and who filled them. And yet without this information a real understanding of political life in the late antebellum South is impossible.

With the hope of filling this gap in our knowledge of southern history the present study was undertaken. Originally, I had hoped to cover the whole of the South, but could soon see that this would be impossible in a single volume. Therefore, I determined to study first those seven states of the lower South which seceded and formed the Southern Confederacy prior to Lincoln's inauguration. My purpose here has been to examine the outer structure of state and county government, for, desirable as an examination of the internal workings of southern government would be, there was much to be learned first about the structure itself. Regrettably, the limits of time and space have prevented a consideration of city and local government. The writer is aware that in some areas, New Orleans and Charleston, for example, city government played a vital part in the lives of southern people; but the lower South was a rural area, and urban affairs were therefore of secondary importance.

The approach employed in this study is similar to that used in my earlier examination of the secession conventions. I have attempted not only to describe the machinery of state and county government in the lower South, but also to examine the characteristics of the individuals who participated in political life in the late antebellum period. In terms of social and economic data, who were these men? Were they simply "slaveholders, and the members of that society which clustered around them," as James Ford Rhodes believed when writing his *History of the United States From the Compromise of 1850*? Or did they come "from the plain people rather than the large planter class," as Fletcher M. Green contended in his article "Democracy in the Old South"?[1] Or were they both planters and plain folk? And what were the differences in the governmental leadership from state to state? Through the approach of collective biography as employed in this study, it is hoped that these and other questions relating to southern government in the late antebellum period may be answered.

Many people have contributed to the completion of the present volume. As in my earlier study of the secession conventions, Professor Barnes F. Lathrop of the University of Texas continued to be a storehouse of information concerning the late antebellum period. His kindness, generosity, and constant willingness to listen to a former student's research prob-

[1] *Journal of Southern History*, XII (January, 1946), 3–23.

lems, both real and imagined, saved the author from many pitfalls and aided immeasurably in the completion of the manuscript.

To Joe B. Frantz, also of the University of Texas, I owe a debt of gratitude for encouragement and advice concerning publication. David Donald of Johns Hopkins, a pioneer in the application of the techniques of collective biography to historical problems, offered valuable comments concerning methodology. Grady McWhiney of the University of British Columbia contributed advice concerning Alabama politics for the period, as did also Edwin Miles of the University of Houston concerning Mississippi politics. One of Professor McWhiney's former students, Richard Beringer, now of California State College at Hayward, contributed a number of bits of information concerning key political figures of the period.

Various individuals at the University of Tennessee provided helpful suggestions. Special thanks in this regard are extended to Dr. Lee S. Greene, head of the political science department, who furnished invaluable advice concerning the manuscript. Not only did Dr. Greene suggest basic organizational changes in the manuscript, but he also willingly and unhesitantly gave much of his valuable time in pointing out how this could be done. He and the University of Tennessee Press provided the type of encouragement that any author needs in preparing a work for publication. I only hope that in some small way this book is worthy of the time and energy they expended in my behalf.

Appreciation is expressed to various librarians and archivists who made my task easier: especially, Miss Maxine Johnston and Mrs. Major Bell, research librarians at Lamar State College; Dr. Llerena Friend, director of the Texas History Center at the

University of Texas; Dr. Dorman Winfrey, director, Texas State Library; Dr. James Day, formerly archivist, Texas State Library; Mr. Chester V. Kielman, archivist, University of Texas; Miss Marcelle F. Schertz, reference archivist, Louisiana State University Library; Mrs. Carl Black, research assistant, Mississippi Department of Archives and History; Mr. Peter A. Brannon, director, Alabama Department of Archives and History; Mrs. Mary Givens Bryan, director, Georgia Department of Archives and History; Dr. Dorothy Dodd, state librarian, Florida; and Mr. Charles E. Lee, director, South Carolina Archives Department.

Many of my colleagues at Lamar aided me in one way or another. Time and space preclude mentioning them all, but special thanks go to Dean Lloyd Cherry, formerly director of the Lamar Research Center; Dr. Earl W. Fornell, member of the Research Committee and professor of government; Dr. Paul Isaac, professor of history; and the late Dr. Samuel Evans, to whom this book is dedicated.

Several student assistants provided invaluable help in reading manuscript census returns and compiling statistical information; among these Martha Payne Leonard, Mary Allbritton Melland, Linda Malin Lang, and Linda Richard deserve particular praise. My secretary for the past two years, Mrs. Connie Garrett, not only aided in typing some of the tables in the appendix, but also relieved me of burdensome administrative chores during the latter stages of my work.

The author received generous financial support from the Lamar Tech Research Center, the Penrose Fund of the American Philosophical Society, and the American Association for State and Local History. Without assistance from these sources my work could not have been completed, and I am extremely appreciative to the administrators of these funds for their faith and confidence.

Finally, I wish to thank members of my family for their patience and understanding. To my wife Edna, who assisted in the preparation of the manuscript as well as sustained me during some moments of discouragement, and to my son Robert, who gave up play time with his father, I express my love.

Beaumont, Texas R.A.W.
June 1, 1968

# CONTENTS

PREFACE *page vii*

LIST OF TABLES *page xv*

☆

THE LEGISLATURE

*Conservative Tradition and Democratic Reform* 3

☆☆

THE GOVERNORS

*Social Leaders in Politics* 48

☆☆☆

COURTS AND JUDGES

*Development of Judicial Systems* 64

☆☆☆☆

THE COUNTIES

*Nineteenth-Century Democracy in Action* 81

☆☆☆☆☆

CLOSE OF AN ERA

*The Lower South on the Eve of War* 107

APPENDIX I

*Personal Characteristics of Southern Legislators* 119

APPENDIX II

*Personal Characteristics of Members of Southern County Governing Boards* 155

BIBLIOGRAPHICAL ESSAY 164

INDEX 181

# LIST OF TABLES

1 Median Age of Members of Southern Legislatures *page 29*

2 Place of Birth of Members of Southern Legislatures *30*

3 Occupations of Members of Southern Legislatures *35*

4 Median Real Property Holding of Members of Southern Legislatures *39*

5 Median Personal Property Holding of Members of Southern Legislatures *40*

6 Slaveholders in Southern Legislatures *41*

7 Property Holding of Political Factions in 1850 Southern Legislatures *45*

8 Real Property Holding of Members of Southern County Governing Bodies, 1860 *99*

9 Personal Property Holding of Members of Southern County Governing Bodies, 1860 *101*

10 Slaveholders in Southern County Governing Bodies, 1860 *103*

# THE PEOPLE IN POWER

☆

# THE LEGISLATURE

## *Conservative Tradition and Democratic Reform*

STRETCHING OVER 1,500 miles from the Pee Dee River of South Carolina to the Rio Grande of Texas, the seven states of the lower South possessed an economic unity in the pre-Civil War decade built around massive production of staple crops, chiefly cotton but also rice and sugar cane, and a political unity in national affairs based upon a determination to resist further compromise on the issue of slavery.[1] Here, where John C. Calhoun, R. Barnwell Rhett, and William L. Yancey were the spokesmen, there developed in the late antebellum period a commonness of purpose and resolution which bound the seven states together and set them apart from the upper South where tobacco, not cotton, was king and where moderation and restraint characterized political leadership. At no time were the differences in attitudes between the two Souths more evident than in the winter months of 1860–61; while the states of the upper South debated and deliberated after Lincoln's election, the states of the lower South seceded and formed the first Southern Confederacy.[2]

[1] The seven states of the lower South produced 88 per cent of the nation's cotton in the late antebellum period. Nearly one fourth was produced in Mississippi alone. Eighth Census of United States, 1860, vol. III, *Agriculture* (Washington, 1864), 185.

[2] An earlier study of the lower South pointing out its distinct features is William G. Brown, *The Lower South in American History* (New York, 1902). An important recent study emphasizing the differences between the upper and lower South is Terry G. Jordan, "The Imprint of the Upper and Lower South on Mid-Nineteenth-Century Texas," *Annals of the Association of American Geographers,* LVII (December, 1967), 667–90.

Geographically the lower South was a land of contrast. The variations in physical size of the seven states were immense; the largest state of the group, Texas, was nearly nine times larger than the smallest, South Carolina, and nearly as large as the other six states combined. Two thirds of the half million square miles that made up the region fronted the Gulf of Mexico, and the other third faced eastward toward the Atlantic. Diversity was evident in the terrain, too. From the long, sandy Coastal Plain of South Carolina the area stretched across the rolling red hills of the Piedmont into the rich black belt of Alabama and the fertile lowlands of the Mississippi valley and from here through the pines of East Texas into the flat prairie country of the Texas plains. But not all was variation. There was a commonness in climate because everywhere in the lower South the growing season was long and the abundant rainfall nurtured the great staple crops which gave the section its identity.

More than four and a half million people lived in the lower South in the pre-Civil War decade. Of these, more than two million, or 46.5 per cent, were Negro slaves, for well over half of the nation's slave population lived in these seven states. Two of the states, South Carolina and Mississippi, had more slaves than whites; and in all but one, Texas, Negroes constituted at least 40 per cent of the total population.[3]

## *General Constitutional Developments*

South Carolina, in the late antebellum period, was the most aristocratic state in the lower South, if indeed not in the entire

[3] Total population in each of the seven states on the eve of the Civil War was South Carolina, 703,708; Georgia, 1,057,286; Florida, 140,424; Alabama, 964,201; Mississippi, 791,305; Louisiana, 708,002; and Texas, 604,215.

nation. The democratic changes which swept across the country in the early nineteenth century as a part of Jacksonian liberalism scarcely touched the Palmetto state; her society continued to be the "stronghold of the land of aristocracy." [4] Here, as perhaps nowhere else in America, with the possible exception of Virginia, political and social power remained in the hands of the rich and well born. The northern traveler, Frederick Law Olmsted, who visited South Carolina in the 1850's, observed that in the state "the Democratic theory of the social organization is everywhere ridiculed and rejected, in public as well as in private, in the forum as well as the newspapers." [5] A later student of Carolina society commented, "As perhaps in no other state, there existed in South Carolina a conscious and militant aristocracy composed of the planting and professional classes—an aristocracy that took pride in its English antecedents, its public service, its standards of conduct and its guardianship of the social order." [6]

A combination of geographic, economic, and political factors militated against any substantial change in South Carolina society and government. The comparative smallness of its region of hills and mountains, where southern protest movements traditionally were spawned, the spread of its cotton culture throughout the entire state, and the argument of its political leaders, particularly John C. Calhoun, that constitutional reform would create internal dissension and weaken the state in its all important controversy with the federal government over state rights—

[4] Green, "Democracy in the Old South," 17. See also Charles S. Sydnor, *The Development of Southern Sectionalism, 1819–1848* (Baton Rouge, 1948), 288.

[5] Frederick L. Olmsted, *A Journey in the Seaboard Slave States* (New York, 1856), 491.

[6] Rosser Taylor, *Ante-Bellum South Carolina: A Social and Cultural History* (*James Sprunt Studies in History and Political Science;* Chapel Hill, 1942), 41.

all served to prevent much serious discussion of constitutional changes.[7] Although the plain folk occasionally attempted to wrest power from the hands of the Tidewater planters, their efforts usually met with little success.[8] Manhood suffrage was granted as early as 1810, and the legislature frequently discussed changes in representation and in the method of choosing Presidential electors,[9] but here, too, virtually no real change occurred. The state continued to be dominated by the plantation aristocracy.

To a degree unequaled in the other southern states of the late antebellum period, the South Carolina legislature was the center of political life in the state, and through the legislature the planters exercised their control over state and local affairs. The Constitution of 1790 under which South Carolinians were governed for more than seventy years created a highly unified, centralized system of government almost entirely devoid of checks and balances. All real power rested in the legislature, which was "a sort of House of Commons in the extent of its

[7] Sydnor, *Development of Southern Sectionalism,* 288; Chauncey S. Boucher, "Sectionalism, Representation, and the Electoral Question in Ante-Bellum South Carolina," *Washington University Studies,* vol. IV (October, 1916), 14–15; and Fletcher M. Green, *Constitutional Development in the South Atlantic States, 1776–1860* (Chapel Hill, 1930), 250.

[8] In his memoirs Professor Frederick A. Porcher of the College of Charleston describes such an attempt which occurred in 1844. On this occasion an ex-overseer named Dennis unsuccessfully attempted to unite low country farmers against planter domination of the legislature. Samuel G. Stoney (ed.), "The Memoirs of Frederick Adolphus Porcher," *South Carolina Historical and Genealogical Magazine,* XLVII (April, 1946), 105.

[9] Green, "Democracy in the Old South," 17; Boucher, "Sectionalism, Representation, and Electoral Question," 16–28, 47–60; Lillian A. Kibler, *Benjamin F. Perry, South Carolina Unionist* (Durham, 1946), 226–30; and Chilton Williamson, *American Suffrage: From Property to Democracy, 1760–1860* (Princeton, 1960), 157. See also a more recent study by William W. Freehling, *Prelude to Civil War: The Nullification Controversy in South Carolina, 1816–1836* (New York, 1966), 89–91.

power."[10] Not only did the legislature have the usual lawmaking powers, but it also elected the governor, Presidential electors, United States senators, state judges, the secretary of state, commissioners of the treasury, the surveyor general, and most local officials. Thus, executive, judicial, and administrative functions of the state government were in the hands of the legislative branch. Too, the legislature quite frequently set the state's course in national politics by adopting resolutions on federal matters and instructing its United States senators on how to vote in the national Congress.[11] Finally, the legislature was a training ground for future congressmen, more than three fourths of South Carolina's representatives in Congress during the 1850's having previously served in the state assembly.[12]

Representation within the all-powerful South Carolina legislature had not changed substantially since the celebrated "compromise of 1808" by which the state constitution was amended to give each election district, except Charleston (which had two), one senator and one representative for each 1/62 of the

[10] William A. Schaper, "Sectionalism and Representation in South Carolina," American Historical Association *Annual Report*, 1900, vol. I (Washington, 1901), 380. For the Constitution of 1790 see Francis N. Thorpe (comp.), *The Federal and State Constitutions, Colonial Charters, and other Organic Laws* (Washington, 1909), VI, 3258–67. The constitution is ably discussed in Columbus Andrews, *Administrative County Government in South Carolina* (Chapel Hill, 1933), 15–16; David D. Wallace, *The History of South Carolina* (New York, 1934), I, 343–51; and Schaper, "Sectionalism and Representation," 379–80.

[11] Sydnor, *Development of Southern Sectionalism*, 45. See Clement Eaton, "Southern Senators and the Right of Instruction, 1789–1860," *Journal of Southern History*, XVIII (August, 1952), 303–19.

[12] Eighteen of the twenty-three congressmen from South Carolina in the 1850's had previously served in the state legislature. *Biographical Directory of the American Congress, 1774–1961* (Washington, 1961). All of the South Carolina delegates to the Montgomery Convention of 1861 had served in the state legislature. See Charles Robert Lee, Jr., *The Confederate Constitutions* (Chapel Hill, 1963), 48–49.

general property tax that it paid and one for each 1/62 of the white population that it contained. Although this "compromise" was a concession to the rapidly growing districts of the up country, the plantation-rich low country parishes continued to dominate the state senate and to exert more influence in the lower house than they were actually entitled to on the basis of the number of their white inhabitants.[13] Despite various protests from the up country, no other basic change in representation within the legislature occurred before the Civil War.

Although an amendment in 1810 gave all free, white adult men, with the exception of paupers and non-commissioned officers and private soldiers of the U.S. Army, the right to vote for members of the South Carolina legislature, individuals not holding a freehold of fifty acres of land or a town lot were required to be resident in their respective election districts for six months; landholders had no residency qualifications to meet.[14] Too, property qualifications for holding office in the state legislature were provided. Even here a distinction was made between residents and nonresidents, nonresidents being required to possess three times as much property as residents to be eligible for either the house or senate. Senate members,

[13] David D. Wallace, *South Carolina: A Short History, 1520–1948* (Chapel Hill, 1948), 73, notes that parishes were created in the South Carolina low country in 1706 and continued to be civil subdivisions until 1865. The term "district" was used for subdivisions in the up country except for the years 1785–99 when "county" was used. For the story of representation in the legislature see Andrews, *Administrative County Government in South Carolina,* 15, and Schaper, "Sectionalism and Representation," 400–37.

[14] Thorpe, *Federal and State Constitutions,* VI, 3267. In fact, prior to 1819 South Carolina landholders could vote in each constituency in which they held property. For more on the struggle for suffrage reform in South Carolina see Williamson, *American Suffrage,* 151–57.

resident or not, were required to hold twice as much property as house members. The constitutional provision called for resident senators to possess a freehold estate of three hundred pounds sterling, and resident representatives a freehold estate of one hundred and fifty pounds sterling; nonresident senators had to have a freehold estate valued at one thousand pounds sterling, and nonresident representatives a freehold estate valued at five hundred pounds sterling.[15]

While South Carolina remained true to the conservative tradition, other states, starting with similar concepts of representation and legislation, advanced on the road taken by Jacksonian Democracy. Typical of this movement were the developments in Georgia, Florida, and, in some respects, Louisiana.

In his study of Georgia and the national crisis of 1850, Richard Shryock noted that the "Empire State of the South" held a position of political and economic pre-eminence among the states of the lower South in the late antebellum period.[16] Economically stronger than any of the other cotton states and boasting an array of distinguished public leaders headed by Howell Cobb, Robert Toombs, Herschel V. Johnson, and Alexander H. Stephens, Georgia exercised a salutary influence over the lower South in the controversy brought about by the Compromise of 1850 and helped to halt the rising tide of southern radicalism in 1851–52.[17]

[15] Thorpe, *Federal and State Constitutions,* VI, 3259–60. Representatives living within the district represented could also qualify if they owned a freehold of five hundred acres and ten slaves free of debt.

[16] Richard Shryock, *Georgia and the Union in 1850* (Durham, 1926), 9. See also Avery Craven, "The South and the Democratic Process," *Alabama Review,* IV (July, 1951), 202–204.

[17] Ralph A. Wooster, *The Secession Conventions of the South* (Princeton, 1962), 80.

Like her neighbor South Carolina, Georgia was governed in the pre-Civil War decade under a constitution adopted in the eighteenth century. But unlike South Carolina, Georgia had a fairly democratic government for several decades. The Georgia Constitution of 1798, though never so aristocratic as that of South Carolina, had contained a number of undemocratic features; but many of these had been changed by constitutional amendments early in the nineteenth century. By the 1820's Georgia was one of the most democratic states in the South.[18]

The question of representation in the state legislature was a lively one in Georgia politics during the early nineteenth century. Under the Constitution of 1798 each county, irrespective of size or population, was entitled to one member in the state senate. Representation in the lower house was based on the so-called "Federal Ratio" by which counties were allotted representation "according to their respective numbers of free white persons and three-fifths of all the people of color." Each county was assured at least one representative; counties having three thousand persons "agreeable to the foregoing plan of enumeration" were entitled to two representatives; counties of seven thousand had three representatives; counties with more than twelve thousand had four representatives.[19] Although there was some complaint from the non-slaveholding areas of the state that the Federal Ratio gave the big slave counties an unfair advantage in the legislature, the most serious problems with this system of representation were the size and expense of

18 Sydnor, *Development of Southern Sectionalism,* 38. For the Georgia Constitution of 1798 and subsequent amendments see Thorpe, *Federal and State Constitutions,* II, 791–809.

19 Thorpe, *Federal and State Constitutions,* II, 791–92.

the law-making body.[20] The rapid increase in the number of counties in the state—from forty-nine in 1820 to ninety-two by 1840—meant that both houses of the assembly were large and unwieldy. This led to agitation for change, resulting in state conventions in 1833 and 1839 which considered the question of representation. In both instances, however, voter dissatisfaction with proposed changes in representation led to the defeat of constitutional amendments, and by 1840 the Georgia house of representatives and senate together totaled three hundred members.[21]

The convention method having failed to reduce the size of the Georgia legislature, the legislature itself took steps to cut down the number of senators and representatives. In 1842 a constitutional amendment was approved which limited the senate to 47 members and the house to 137. This amendment, ratified the following year, divided the state into forty-seven

[20] Albert B. Saye, *A Constitutional History of Georgia, 1732–1945* (Athens, 1945), 169–70. Professor Paul Murray in his *The Whig Party in Georgia, 1825–1853* (*James Sprunt Studies in History and Political Science;* Chapel Hill, 1948), 39, points out, "The Federal Ratio was hardly worthy of the political action which centered around it in Georgia. Without regard for slave population, the ratio of representation to white population of counties varied from 1/600 to 1/2700. It was true, however, that the Federal Ratio gave an extra representative to some slave counties. But its practical statewide effect was to restore to the counties of large population the representation taken from them by their smaller ratio of representation to white population."

[21] L. E. Roberts, "Sectional Factors in the Movement for Legislative Reapportionment and Reduction in Georgia, 1776–1860," in James C. Bonner and Lucien E. Roberts, *Studies in Georgia History and Government* (Athens, 1940), 117–20; Green, *Constitutional Development,* 233–40; James C. Bonner, "Legislative Apportionment and County Voting in Georgia since 1777," *Georgia Historical Quarterly,* XLVII (December, 1963), 355–56. There were a number of inequalities in the proposed amendments, and, too, the issues became involved in partisan political disagreements dividing the unionist and state rights factions within the state. See Murray, *The Whig Party in Georgia,* 40–41, 49–54, 81–84; Edward M. Steel, Jr., *T. Butler King of Georgia* (Athens, 1964), 20–21; and Jean A. Garrett, "Amendments and Proposed Amendments to the Constitution of 1798" (M.A. thesis, University of Georgia, 1944).

senatorial districts, each composed of two contiguous counties, with one senator from each. It also provided that every county would have at least one representative, that the thirty-seven counties with the greatest population (counting all free white persons and three fifths of the colored population) would have two representatives, and that no county would have more than two members in the lower house. This fixed ratio and fixed number of house members could not be maintained, however, if new counties were to be admitted; consequently, in the 1850's an amendment eliminated the provision calling for a fixed number of representatives. Senatorial districts were also abolished in the 1850's, and each county was again given one senator. With the admission of thirty-nine new counties during this decade, the number of members in the legislature once more neared three hundred. In 1859, Governor Joseph E. Brown urged reduction in the size of the body, but when the war came the legislature was still unwieldy in size.[22]

Few restrictions existed for those who would elect the Georgia legislature. Eligible to vote were all male citizens of the state who were twenty-one years of age, who had resided in the county for six months, and who had "paid such taxes as were required of them, and which they may have had an opportunity of paying, agreeable to law, for the year preceding the election."[23] The Constitution of 1789 had provided for voting by ballot, but the Constitution of 1798 declared, "In all

[22] Roberts, "Sectional Factors in Movements for Legislative Reapportionment," 122; Saye, *Constitutional History of Georgia,* 174; Thorpe, *Federal and State Constitutions,* II, 808–809.

[23] Thorpe, *Federal and State Constitutions,* II, 800. The previous constitution, that of 1789, had made similar provision but with slightly different wording: "and have paid tax for the year preceding the election." *Ibid.,* 789. See also Williamson, *American Suffrage,* 131–32.

elections by the people the electors shall vote *viva voce* until the legislature shall otherwise direct." The next legislature, however, moved quickly to restore the older system, passing in 1799 an act which provided for voting by ballot.

Constitutional requirements for membership in the Georgia legislature were simple. A senator must have reached the age of twenty-five, have been nine years a citizen of the United States and three years an inhabitant of Georgia, and have resided one year immediately preceding his election within the county he represented. A member of the lower house was required to be twenty-one years old, to have been seven years a citizen of the United States, three years an inhabitant of Georgia, and to have resided one year immediately preceding his election in the county which he represented. Originally, a property qualification existed for members of both houses: senators were required to hold an estate valued at five hundred dollars, or taxable property of one thousand dollars within the county of election; and representatives were required to hold an estate valued at two hundred and fifty dollars, or taxable property of five hundred dollars within the county of election. Such restrictions were anachronisms in the Jacksonian age, and in 1835 the constitution was amended to exclude all property qualifications for legislative membership.[24]

Like her northern neighbor Georgia, Florida also made strides toward democracy in the pre-Civil War period. Florida, however, began statehood with a progressive constitution. She was not admitted as a state until 1845 when the tide of change was high. The governor and members of the legislature were elected by the people, and no property qualifications for voting

[24] Thorpe, *Federal and State Constitutions,* II, 791–92, 805–806; Ethel K. Ware, *A Constitutional History of Georgia* (New York, 1947), 80.

or holding office existed. Supreme and circuit court judges were originally appointed by the legislature, but this was later changed to provide for popular election.[25] County commissioners, the most important local officers, had also been selected by the assembly during the territorial period, but one of the first acts of the new state legislature was to grant this power to the people.[26] By 1860 the only undemocratic feature in her government was the manner of apportionment for representation in the lower house of the legislature. Florida had, like Georgia, retained the so-called Federal Ratio, a system whereby three fifths of the Negro slaves were counted in computing population figures, thus giving the plantation counties more strength in the state legislature. But otherwise, Floridians in the late antebellum period enjoyed full democracy in the nineteenth-century sense.

Both suffrage and officeholding requirements were simple in early Florida. The Constitution of 1838, under which Floridians were governed until the Reconstruction era, granted suffrage to all free white males, except federal military personnel, who were twenty-one years of age and had resided in the state for one year and in the county for six months prior to election.[27] Requirements for officeholding were slightly more

[25] Edwin Lacy Williams, Jr., "Florida in the Union, 1845–1861" (Ph.D. dissertation, University of North Carolina, 1951), 60.

[26] See Thorpe, *Federal and State Constitutions,* II, 673; *Florida Acts* (1845), 32–33.

[27] The Constitution of 1838 originally required two years' residency in the state, but in 1847 this was reduced to one year. Thorpe, *Federal and State Constitutions*, II, 673, 685–86; and Leslie A. Thompson, *A Manual or Digest of the Statute Law of the State of Florida* (Boston, 1847), 65–66. For the Constitution of 1838 see Sidney W. Martin, *Florida During Territorial Days* (Athens, Ga., 1944), 266–72; James B. Whitfield, "Florida's First Constitution," *Florida Historical Quarterly,* XVII (October, 1938), 73–83; and F. W. Hoskins, "The St. Joseph Convention," *Florida Historical Quarterly,* XVI (July–October, 1937), 33–43, 95–109.

restrictive but still relatively uncomplicated. The governor was required to be thirty years of age, a citizen of the United States for ten years or an inhabitant of Florida at the time of adoption of the state constitution, and a resident of Florida for five years prior to election. State senators had to be twenty-five years of age, United States citizens, and residents of the state for two years and of the district for one year prior to election. Members of the lower house had to meet the same citizenship and residency requirements as did senators but could qualify at the age of twenty-one. The constitution specifically prohibited bank officers, ministers of the gospel, and those who engaged in duels from serving in the legislature or governor's chair.[28]

Louisiana, like most southern states, made some democratic advances in the first half of the nineteenth century by reducing barriers to voting and officeholding and increasing the number of offices filled by popular election. But, as in Georgia and Florida, Louisiana maintained elements of an earlier conservatism by basing representation in the legislature on total population, thus giving the large slave parishes a disproportionate share of votes in the state assembly, the most powerful instrument of state government.

The Constitution of 1812, under which Louisianians were governed for thirty-three years, limited suffrage to adult, white males who had purchased public land or paid state taxes. Small as this property requirement may seem, "it placed the ballot chiefly in the hands of landowners and shopkeepers, and never admitted to the polls more than a third of the adult freemen."[29] Furthermore, these voters were restricted in the

[28] Thorpe, *Federal and State Constitutions,* II, 666, 669, 673–74, 683.

[29] Roger W. Shugg, "Suffrage and Representation in Ante-Bellum Louisiana," *Louisiana Historical Quarterly,* XIX (April, 1936), 390. See also Melvin Evans, *A*

election of governors to candidates whose landed estates were valued at $5,000, in the election of senators to those whose landed estates were valued at $1,000, and to representatives whose landed estates were valued at $500.

According to the Constitution of 1812, representation in Louisiana was to be "equal and uniform" but based upon the number of qualified electors rather than upon total white population. The constitution made the first assignment of representatives and directed the legislature to take a census in 1813 and every fourth year thereafter for purposes of reapportionment. Although several such reapportionments were made in the early years of statehood, there continued to be a number of inequities in house representation, even on the basis of qualified electors. The problem was even more acute in the senate because the constitution provided "the state shall be divided into fourteen senatorial districts, which shall forever remain indivisible."[30] Thus, as some districts grew rapidly in population and qualified electors, their representation in the upper house remained unchanged. By 1840, for example, New Orleans had one third of the state's population and nearly one fourth of the qualified electors but elected only two senators. On the other hand, nine other districts with about the same portion of the state's population and only slightly more electors chose nine senators.[31]

---

*Study in the State Government of Louisiana* (Baton Rouge, 1932), 29; and Thorpe, *Federal and State Constitutions,* III, 1381–82.

30 Thorpe, *Federal and State Constitutions,* III, 1382.

31 And of course the inequity is even greater if one considers the total white population, 21.5 per cent of which lived in the nine districts and 40.6 per cent in New Orleans. Emmett Asseff, *Legislative Apportionment in Louisiana* (Baton Rouge, 1950), 12; and Roger W. Shugg, *Origins of Class Struggle in Louisiana* (Baton Rouge, 1939), 122.

The winds of reform of the second quarter of the nineteenth century brought changes to Louisiana. Dissatisfaction with the aristocratic features of the old constitution led upstate Democrats to work feverishly for constitutional revision, resulting in the convention of 1845 that drafted a new basic document for the state. The new constitution, which served the people of Louisiana for only seven years but formed the model for all later revisions, was in many ways a democratic document. Not only did it create more elective offices, prohibit monopolies and special charters, and provide for free public education, but it also abolished all property qualifications for voting and officeholding. So strong was the feeling against property and tax restrictions that attempts to levy a poll tax were defeated by overwhelming votes. The convention did, however, raise the residency requirements for voting from one to two years—an effort to curb the political activities of the thousands of immigrants who were pouring into New Orleans.[32]

In one important respect, that of legislative representation, the Constitution of 1845 was a disappointment to the champions of democracy. They had hoped that the basis of apportionment might be changed from qualified electors to total *white* population. Instead, a compromise was worked out between the delegates from New Orleans and those from the "black belt" parishes (with 50 per cent or more of slaves in the total population) whereby apportionment of representatives in the lower house continued to be based upon the number of qualified voters. However, this time no limit was placed on the maximum number of representatives per parish, a restriction

[32] Shugg, *Origins of Class Struggle in Louisiana,* 128. There is a thorough analysis of the drafting of the Constitution of 1845 in Francis N. Thorpe, *A Constitutional History of the American People* (New York, 1898), I, 400–86.

which had been feared by heavily populated and rapidly growing New Orleans. On the other hand, apportionment of senators was henceforth based on total population, a provision which pleased the great slave parishes. As Roger Shugg has said of the New Orleans and black belt delegates who made this compromise possible, "It was not what either most desired, but rather the best that both could get." [33] Under this arrangement, New Orleans, with her twenty representatives, continued to hold the balance of power in the lower house, and the conservative slave parishes, with only a third of the white population but nearly two thirds of the senators, completely dominated the upper house.[34]

Although the 1845 Louisiana constitution was considered a marked improvement over the old constitution, dissatisfaction with the new document prevailed in a number of areas. Many felt that all executive and judicial offices should be elective. Others objected to the new residency requirements which restricted the political activities of not only the newly arrived immigrants but also the mechanics, laborers, and other poor whites who moved frequently. And Whig businessmen wished to throw off the newly imposed constitutional shackles placed upon banking and railroad expansion.[35] As a result, the movement for a new fundamental law gained rapid momentum, and in 1852 another constitutional convention was held.

[33] Shugg, *Origins of Class Struggle in Louisiana,* 133.

[34] Asseff, *Legislative Apportionment in Louisiana,* 17–18; Thorpe, *Federal and State Constitutions,* III, 1394–95, 1408–1409.

[35] Shugg, *Origins of Class Struggle in Louisiana,* 130–36; James K. Greer, *Louisiana Politics, 1845–1861* (Baton Rouge, 1930; reprinted from *Louisiana Historical Quarterly, XII–XIII*), 89–92; Leslie M. Norton, "A History of the Whig Party in Louisiana" (Ph.D. dissertation, Louisiana State University, 1940), 338–39; and William H. Adams, III, "The Louisiana Whig Party" (Ph.D. dissertation, Louisiana State University, 1960), 284–85.

The constitution drafted by the convention of 1852 was in some respects an advance in democracy. Residency requirements for voting were reduced from the two years imposed in 1845 to one year; age, citizenship, and residency restrictions for the governorship were reduced substantially; judges of the supreme and inferior courts, the secretary of state, state treasurer, and attorney general all became elective officials; and the process for constitutional amendment was made easier.[36] So sweeping were the changes that one New Orleans paper referred to the new document as "liberal, democratic, and radical."[37]

But the new "liberal, democratic, and radical" constitution was actually a victory for the state's conservative forces. Under the leadership of Judah P. Benjamin, the Whig-dominated convention made generous provisions for the creation of corporations, banks, and railroads and removed constitutional restrictions created by the earlier body. Then the convention moved to make certain that both houses of the state's most powerful branch of government, the legislature, would be in the hands of the propertied classes. The previous constitution had transferred control of the upper house to the heavily slave-populated areas of the state by basing senatorial apportionment on total population; the convention of 1852 completed the process by applying this principle to the lower house as well. As a result of this action and subsequent apportionment in 1854 and 1859, the state's black belt parishes, with slightly less than one third of the white population, elected over one half of the state's lawmakers. Louisiana's great planters and their merchant-lawyer allies were thus firmly in the

[36] Thorpe, *Federal and State Constitutions,* III, 1393–1402, 1411–21, 1426–27.
[37] New Orleans *Weekly Delta,* August 15, 1852.

saddle of the state's governmental activities as the antebellum period drew to a close.[38]

Modern readers may well be surprised that the two states of the deep South which led in democratic reform were Alabama and Mississippi. Indeed, Alabama had been a leader in the movement for political democracy since her admission as a state in 1819. Her first state constitution, under which Alabamians were governed until Reconstruction, was at the time of adoption the most democratic in the entire South. A "mixture of liberalism and conservatism, the product of the past as well as a forerunner of the future,"[39] the Constitution of 1819 was quite advanced for the time and gave political control of both state and county government to the people of Alabama. All adult white males who met a residence requirement of one year in the state could vote or hold office; all property, tax-paying, and militia requirements were abolished. With the exception of the judiciary, state and county offices were made elective, and the white basis rather than the Federal Ratio was adopted for representation in the state legislature.[40]

The Constitution of 1819 further provided that elections and sessions of the legislature were to be held annually. Members of the house of representatives served one-year terms, and members of the senate served three-year terms. Almost immediately, however, agitation for biennial sessions and elections began. Under an amendment submitted to the people in 1830,

[38] Shugg, *Origins of Class Struggle in Louisiana,* 139. See also Asseff, *Legislative Apportionment in Louisiana,* 20–26; Norton, "A History of the Whig Party in Louisiana," 340–42; and Greer, *Louisiana Politics, 1845–1861,* 93–94.

[39] Malcolm Cook McMillan, "The Alabama Constitution of 1819: A Study of Constitution-Making on the Frontier," *Alabama Review,* III (October, 1950), 283.

[40] *Ibid.,* 283; Thomas P. Abernethy, *The Formative Period in Alabama, 1815–1828* (Montgomery, 1922), 43.

elections and sessions would be held every other year; representatives would serve two-year terms and senators would serve four. The proposal was defeated in 1830, but the issue did not die. In 1845 the people accepted a similar amendment, and it became effective the following year.[41]

Constitutional requirements for membership in the Alabama legislature were simple. No property or tax qualification for voting or holding office existed. Both senators and representatives were required to be white males, citizens of the United States, residents of the state two years and of the county or district one year. Representatives had to be twenty-one years of age, and senators had to be twenty-seven.[42] Representation in both houses was based upon white population only, and the constitution required periodic reapportionment of the legislature, a provision which was carried out by legislation without the constant fights so common in many southern states.[43]

Mississippi was even more democratic in her form of government than Alabama. With the adoption of a new constitution in 1832, Mississippi became the most democratic state in the entire South, a position she maintained throughout the late antebellum period. Not only did the new constitution provide

[41] Malcolm Cook McMillan, *Constitutional Development in Alabama, 1798–1901: A Study in Politics, the Negro, and Sectionalism* (*James Sprunt Studies in History and Political Science;* Chapel Hill, 1955), 51–55. See Thorpe, *Federal and State Constitutions,* I, 115, for the amendment.

[42] Thorpe, *Federal and State Constitutions,* I, 99–101.

[43] McMillan, *Constitutional Development in Alabama,* 70–71. The Democrat-dominated legislature also abolished the use of the three-fifths ratio in the elections of federal congressmen, thus reducing the power of the black belt, the Whig stronghold. The gerrymandering of congressional districts also aided the Democrats in controlling these districts. See Frank L. Owsley, *Plain Folk of the Old South* (Baton Rouge, 1949), 142.

suffrage for all adult white males and eliminate all property, tax, and militia requirements for voting and officeholding, but it also replaced the undemocratic county courts with boards of police whose members were popularly elected. All executive offices of the state, including secretary of state, treasurer, and auditor of public accounts, were made elective; and the people were granted the right to elect all their judges—even the members of the High Court of Errors and Appeals—a step which no other southern state had taken at the time.[44]

Mississippi's liberal Constitution of 1832 was the result of several complex factors: "the desire for local or sectional advantage on the part of the newer regions of the state; the forces of Jacksonian democracy, at work in the older parts of the state as well as in the frontier regions; [and] the dissatisfaction with certain specific, though not necessarily undemocratic features of the old constitution."[45] The previous constitution, that of 1817, had made no provision for amendment except by the summoning of a new convention. By 1832 it had become abundantly clear that the state needed a new constitution. In the spring of that year, elections were held for delegates to a constitutional convention, and in the fall the convention drafted the new constitution.[46]

The new Mississippi constitution removed all restrictions to white male suffrage. Section 20 of the Declaration of Rights

[44] Sydnor, *Development of Southern Sectionalism,* 283–84. For a thorough study of the Constitution of 1832 see Winbourne Magruder Drake, "Constitutional Development in Mississippi, 1817–1865" (Ph.D. dissertation, University of North Carolina, 1954), 129–77.

[45] Winbourne Magruder Drake, "The Mississippi Constitutional Convention of 1832," *Journal of Southern History,* XXIII (August, 1957), 368–69.

[46] Edwin A. Miles, *Jacksonian Democracy in Mississippi* (*James Sprunt Studies in History and Political Science;* Chapel Hill, 1960), 35.

specifically stated that "no property qualification for eligibility to office, or for the right of suffrage, shall ever be required by law in this State"; Section 1 of Article III provided that "every free white male person of the age of twenty-one years or upwards, who shall be a citizen of the United States, and shall have resided in this State one year preceding an election, and the last four months within the county, city, or town in which he offers to vote, shall be deemed a qualified elector."[47] The constitution allowed any otherwise qualified voter who had just moved to a new county to vote for state and district officers and members of Congress.[48]

There were no property, tax, or militia requirements for membership in the Mississippi legislature, and representation was based upon the total white population. Representatives were required to meet a two-year state and a one-year county residency requirement and had to be at least twenty-one years of age. Senators were required to show a four-year state and a one-year district residency and could not run until they were thirty years of age. Representatives served for two years, and senators four; regular sessions of the legislature were on a biennial basis, although special sessions were by no means uncommon.[49]

Although Texas has definite western characteristics, it is also

[47] Thorpe, *Federal and State Constitutions,* IV, 2050–51.

[48] *Ibid.,* IV, 2051–52. Drake, "Mississippi Constitutional Convention of 1832," 362, notes that additional efforts at liberalizing residency requirements were blocked by delegates from the southern counties who did not want to increase or facilitate legislative representation of the newer counties.

[49] Miles, *Jacksonian Democracy in Mississippi,* 41, points out that from 1833 to 1842 there were no fewer than eleven sessions of the legislature. Thorpe, *Federal and State Constitutions,* IV, 2052–53, gives requirements for members of the legislature. The Constitution of 1832 also provided for periodic reapportionment of the legislature.

a southern state and, along with Mississippi and Alabama, was a leader in the southern movement for political democracy. Almost from the moment of independence from Mexico, Texans had charted a steady course in nineteenth-century liberalism. Through the period of the republic and on into statehood, through two constitutions and amendments thereto, the movement to break down all barriers to popular rule had proceeded. The constitutions of 1836 and 1845 provided for the popular election of the governor and legislators, and amendments in 1850 provided for the election of judges and most executive officers. There were no property or militia restrictions to voting or officeholding, and residency requirements were not overly burdensome. Apportionment in the lower house of the legislature was based on white population and in the upper house on the number of qualified electors; reapportionment was regularly undertaken and was basically fair.[50]

The Constitution of 1845, under which Texans were governed in the pre-Civil War decade, was "well designed and well written."[51] Modeled largely upon the Constitution of the Republic (1836) but influenced also by the newly completed Louisiana constitution, the 1845 Texas constitution ideally suited the spirit of Texans of the mid-nineteenth century. In it

[50] Reapportionment laws were passed in 1848, 1853, and 1860. H. P. N. Gammel, *The Laws of Texas, 1822–1897* (Austin, 1898), III, 311–16; IV, 1289–94, 1402–1408. The decision to base apportionment in the upper house upon qualified electors rather than the total white population was a concession to the frontier areas of the state where there were fewer children and women. See also Thorpe, *Federal and State Constitutions,* VI, 3547–68; Frederic L. Paxson, "The Constitution of Texas, 1845," *Southwestern Historical Quarterly,* XVIII (April, 1915), 386–98; and Annie Laura Middleton, "The Formation of the Texas Constitution of 1845" (M.A. thesis, University of Texas, 1920), for constitutional provisions.

[51] Rupert N. Richardson, *Texas, the Lone Star State* (Englewood Cliffs, N.J., 1958), 126.

were expressed buoyant optimism and exuberant confidence in the common man, along with a simplicity soon to pass with the growing complexity of society. Much was said in the 1845 document about the rights of man; comparatively little was said about banking, incorporation, and property rights.[52] Voting and officeholding requirements were simple. All free adult males who were citizens of the United States or the Republic of Texas, and who resided in the state one year and in the county six months prior to election, were entitled to vote. Indians who paid no taxes and Africans and their descendants were specifically excluded from voting.[53] As in the case of other states, military personnel of the federal government were ineligible to vote. Qualifications for officeholding were basically the same as for voting, although some offices had special requirements in respect to age and residency. Ministers of the gospel were specifically barred from serving in the legislature, and duelists were excluded from all public offices.[54]

## *Legislative Power*

In American political theory, the state legislature, in spite of the tradition of separation of powers, is the residuary legatee of state government. The memory of the colonial governor led to a history of constitutionally powerful state legislatures, a history which was persistent whether the state was conservative or democratic. In Florida, for example, the most powerful

[52] Paxson, "The Constitution of Texas, 1845," 398.

[53] Paxson, *ibid.,* 392, points out that an early draft of the Constitution of 1845 had provided that "free white males" were eligible to vote, but objection was raised to this because of doubt prevailing among some Texans as to the color of Mexicans. So the word "white" was struck out, and a phrase was added barring Indians and Negroes.

[54] Thorpe, *Federal and State Constitutions,* VI, 3549–52, 3560.

branch of government was the legislative. Here the significant issues of the day—the tariff, banking, and internal improvements—were all discussed, debated, and, in part, resolved. And here some of the state's future congressmen, governors, and state judges gained their first experience in state affairs. Usually this was true of other states. The legislature was the dominant branch of government in Georgia. Under the Constitution of 1798 the legislature not only made all laws and ordinances, levied taxes, and selected and instructed United States senators, but also elected the governor, secretary of state, surveyor general, adjutant general, general officers of the militia, and judges of the superior and inferior courts. It was also the training ground for Georgians in national government, thirty-four of the thirty-seven Georgia congressmen in the 1850's having earlier served in the state legislature.[55]

Over the years some legislatures tended to lose certain powers. In Georgia, for example, constitutional amendments adopted in the nineteenth century reduced the scope of legislative activity by giving the voters rather than the legislature the right to choose most of the executive officers of the state.[56] Changes of this type occurred in other states as well.

Nevertheless, in all seven states of the lower South, from the most democratic to the most aristocratic, the legislature continued to be the most important branch of government in the antebellum period. To be sure, considerable variations in the role played by the legislature existed: in South Carolina it was

[55] Based upon information found in *Biographical Directory of the American Congress.* Seven of Georgia's ten delegates to the Montgomery Convention in 1861 had previously served in the state legislature. Lee, *Confederate Constitutions,* 157.

[56] See Thorpe, *Federal and State Constitutions,* II, 791–802; and Saye, *Constitutional History of Georgia,* 165–68.

*the* government, electing governors, judges, and Presidential electors and directing state and county affairs through special legislative commissions, whereas in democratic Mississippi its powers were confined almost exclusively to the law-making area. Too, there were some restrictions in legislative powers, partly as a result of new constitutions which specifically limited legislative action in such areas as banking, corporations, slaves, and public indebtedness, and partly because more power was being turned over directly to the people.[57] But even so, on the eve of the Civil War the legislature remained the center of governmental activity in all the states of the lower South.

## *The Occupations and Characteristics of Legislators*

What of the men who served as southern legislators? Generally speaking they were middle-aged planters, farmers, or lawyers, holders of property, including slaves, who were born in the slaveholding states and usually in the lower South.

South Carolina, by most touchstones, should be considered the most conservative state. In that commonwealth, the bulk of delegates to the thirty-ninth (1850–51) and forty-fourth (1860–61) legislatures were middle-aged, South Carolina-born planters and farmers. Most of the members were holders of substantial real and personal property, and four out of five were slaveholders. A number of lawyers and physicians and some trades people served, but the majority of legislators belonged to the landed gentry.[58]

[57] Green, *Constitutional Development,* 302–303.

[58] See Harold S. Schultz, *Nationalism and Sectionalism in South Carolina, 1852–1860* (Durham, 1950), 5, for a description of social aspects of government service in South Carolina. Many considered service in the legislature a civic duty, perhaps accounting for a rapid turnover in legislative personnel. In 1860, for example,

The median age for membership in the two South Carolina legislatures was slightly higher in the senate in both cases.[59] This, of course, is partly to be expected because of the nature of the two bodies and because of a constitutional requirement setting a thirty-year minimum age for members of the senate and only a twenty-one year minimum for house members. Furthermore, an overwhelming majority of South Carolina legislators in both 1850 and 1860 were born in that state—91.8 per cent of all members of the thirty-ninth legislature for whom place of birth could be determined and 93.0 per cent of the forty-fourth legislature.[60]

Personal characteristics of Georgia legislators were similar to those of South Carolina. In two Georgia legislatures of the late antebellum period, those of 1849–50 and 1859–60, the average legislator was about forty years of age. House members were slightly younger than senate members, the median age being

sixty-four members of the house and sixteen members of the senate had no previous service. The Charleston *Daily Courier,* October 27, 1858, reported that the forty-third assembly had seventy-four new house and seventeen new senate members.

[59] Information for members of the South Carolina legislature is based primarily upon the manuscript returns of the Seventh and Eighth Censuses of the United States, 1850 and 1860, but supplemented by data taken from *Cyclopedia of Eminent and Representative Men of the Carolinas of the Nineteenth Century . . .* (Madison, 1892), I; *Charleston Directory Containing the Names of the Inhabitants . . .* (Charleston, 1859); J. C. Hemphill (ed.), *Men of Mark in South Carolina* (Washington, 1907), I; Emily Bellinger Reynolds and Joan Reynolds Faunt (comps.), *Biographical Directory of the Senate of South Carolina, 1776–1964* (Columbia, 1964); John A. May and Joan Reynolds Faunt, *South Carolina Secedes* (Columbia, 1960); John B. O'Neall, *Biographical Sketches of the Bench and Bar of South Carolina* (Charleston, 1859); and Ralph Wooster, "Membership of the South Carolina Secession Convention," *South Carolina Historical Magazine,* LV (October, 1954), 191–97.

[60] South Carolina attracted few immigrants; 96.6 per cent of the entire 1860 population of the state had been born in South Carolina. Eighth Census of United States, vol. I, *Population* (Washington, 1864), 473. See also Alfred Glaze Smith, Jr., *Economic Readjustment of an Old Cotton State: South Carolina, 1820–1860* (Columbia, 1958), 19–44.

39 years in 1850 and 40 years in 1860. Senate medians for the same years were 41 and 42.5 years, respectively.[61]

Two thirds, or 66.8 per cent, of the 1850 legislators were native Georgians; 105 of the 157 located in the federal census

TABLE I

MEDIAN AGE OF MEMBERS OF SOUTHERN LEGISLATURES

| *Legislature* | *1850* | *1860* |
|---|---|---|
| South Carolina | House 39<br>Senate 45 | House 39<br>Senate 45 |
| Georgia | House 39<br>Senate 41 | House 40<br>Senate 42.5 |
| Florida | Not<br>Determined | House 39<br>Senate 38 |
| Alabama | House 39<br>Senate 43 | House 40<br>Senate 43 |
| Mississippi | House 38<br>Senate 38 | House 40<br>Senate 45 |
| Louisiana | House 39<br>Senate 42 | House 41<br>Senate 43 |
| Texas | House 35<br>Senate 38 | House 41<br>Senate 42 |

for that year listed Georgia as place of birth. An even higher percentage of native sons served in the 1860 legislature; 198 of the 267 legislators for whom places of birth could be determined, or 74.2 per cent, named Georgia as their place of

[61] Social and economic data for members of the Georgia legislatures of 1849–50 and 1859–60 are taken primarily from the manuscript returns of the Seventh and Eighth Censuses of the United States, 1850 and 1860.

TABLE 2

PLACE OF BIRTH OF MEMBERS OF SOUTHERN LEGISLATURES

| *Legislature* | *Place of Birth* | *Percentages* 1850 | 1860 |
|---|---|---|---|
| South Carolina | Lower South | 92.3 | 94.2 |
| | Upper South | 3.5 | 3.8 |
| | North | 2.8 | .7 |
| | Foreign | 1.4 | 1.3 |
| Georgia | Lower South | 81.5 | 85.7 |
| | Upper South | 18.5 | 12.3 |
| | North | — | .8 |
| | Foreign | — | 1.2 |
| Florida | Lower South | Not Determined | 77.1 |
| | Upper South | | 16.6 |
| | North | | 4.2 |
| | Foreign | | 2.1 |
| Alabama | Lower South | 62.1 | 75.6 |
| | Upper South | 30.7 | 22.7 |
| | North | 4.8 | 1.7 |
| | Foreign | 2.4 | — |
| Mississippi | Lower South | 52.1 | 58.1 |
| | Upper South | 41.1 | 40.5 |
| | North | 3.7 | 1.3 |
| | Foreign | 3.1 | — |
| Louisiana | Lower South | 53.5 | 61.2 |
| | Upper South | 31.4 | 24.5 |
| | North | 10.5 | 9.1 |
| | Foreign | 4.6 | 5.2 |
| Texas | Lower South | 28.4 | 34.2 |
| | Upper South | 58.2 | 50.0 |
| | North | 10.5 | 11.7 |
| | Foreign | 2.9 | 4.1 |

birth.[62] In the 1850 legislature all members whose place of birth could be determined came from four southern states: Georgia, North Carolina, South Carolina, and Virginia. Membership in the 1860 body was, however, slightly more cosmopolitan, for though the vast majority still came from the aforementioned states, two members were born in Tennessee, two in Kentucky, and one each in Massachusetts, New York, England, Ireland, and France.

The story was similar in Alabama. There the overwhelming majority of legislators in both 1850 and 1860 were persons born in the slaveholding states. One hundred and fifteen of the 124 members of the 1850 legislature whose place of birth could be determined, or 92.8 per cent, were born in the South. Seventy-seven were born in the lower South and thirty-eight in the upper and border South. Six members of the 1850 legislature were born in northern states, and three in foreign countries. The percentage of non-southerners, however, was steadily declining, and only two members of the 1860 legislature were born outside the South. The number of legislators born in the upper South was also declining; only twenty-seven of the 117 southern-born members in the 1860 legislature were from the upper or border slaveholding states.

In Mississippi, too, most of the members of both the 1850 and 1860 legislatures were born in slaveholding states. Even here, however, slight differences in the two bodies are noticeable. In 1850 fifty-six of the 107 legislators whose place of birth could be determined, or 52.3 per cent, were born in the lower South; forty-four members, or 41.1 per cent, were born in the

[62] Nearly four out of five residents of Georgia in the late antebellum period had been born in the state, 79.9 per cent of the free population as determined by the federal census. Eighth Census of United States, 1860, vol. I, *Population,* 76.

upper South. Four members of the Mississippi legislature of 1850 were born in northern states and three in foreign countries. In 1860 only one member of the legislature, Representative Charles Clark of Bolivar County, had been born outside the South. He was a native of Ohio.

More than half of the members of the 1850 and 1860 Louisiana legislatures were born in the lower South, the figures being forty-six of the eighty-six members in 1850, or 53.5 per cent, and sixty of the ninety-eight members in 1860, or 61.2 per cent. In both years Louisiana led as the place of birth for the most legislators, 33.7 per cent of the 1850 members and 38.8 per cent of the 1860 members listing Louisiana as their native state. Nearly a third of the 1850 legislators, 31.4 per cent, were born in the upper South, but this dropped to one fourth, 24.5 per cent, in the 1860 lawmaking body. Nine legislators in 1850 and nine in 1860 were born in northern states, while four in 1850 and five in 1860 were born in foreign countries.

Texas differed slightly from the normal pattern. It was a young state and had attracted immigrants, and most of its legislators (in 1849–50 and 1859–60) were in their thirties and forties. Members of the 1850 Texas legislature were quite young, the median of thirty-six years being the lowest found in the seven states. Only six members of that body were fifty years of age or older, and only one of these, Jesse Grimes, was venerable enough to be in his sixties. Although most members of the two legislatures were born in slaveholding states, a greater portion of them came from states of the upper South than from states of the lower South.[63] Thirty-nine legislators in 1850, or

[63] There were slightly more Texans in the total population born in the states of the upper South than in the lower South, if native-born Texans are not included. If the 153,043 native-born Texans are included, however, there were one and one-half

58.2 per cent, and fifty-five in 1860, or 50.0 per cent, were born in states of the upper South. Nineteen Texas legislators in 1850 and thirty-eight in 1860 were born in the lower South. Seven legislators in 1850 and thirteen in 1860 were born outside the United States. Tennessee was the birthplace of more immigrants in the Texas population than any other state and was the leading place of birth for legislators in both 1850 and 1860. There were no Alabamians in the 1850 body and only eight in the 1860 assembly, even though that state ranked second as a birthplace for immigrants to Texas. North Carolina, on the other hand, which ranked seventh as a place of birth for Texans, furnished seventeen legislators, and Virginia, which ranked eleventh, furnished twenty for the same period. No native-born Texans sat in the 1850 legislature, but there were five in the 1860 body.

Slightly more than half the legislators in the lower South were farmers or planters, unsurprisingly, given the character of the area. Nearly one fourth of the legislators were lawyers, and approximately one fifth came from a wide range of occupational groups including merchants, physicians, teachers, craftsmen, and occasionally mechanics or laborers. Generally they were also property holders.

By constitutional requirement all legislators in South Carolina had to own property. Although this requirement was not adhered to rigidly, most legislators whose names were located in Schedule No. 1 on the manuscript federal census were listed with property. The median for real property holders was greater for senators than for representatives, $11,000 for senate members in 1850 and $25,000 in 1860, compared to $8,000 in

times as many Texas residents of 1860 born in the lower South as in the upper South. Eighth Census of the United States, vol. I, *Population,* 490.

1850 and $10,000 in 1860 for house members. Former governor John L. Manning, who sat briefly in the forty-fourth senate and for whom the census listed $1,256,000 in real property, was the wealthiest person to serve in either of the two South Carolina legislatures. Joshua J. Ward, senator from All Saints' parish and for whom the census listed $587,500 in real property, was the only other legislator to hold more than half a million dollars in real property. Eleven of the thirteen individuals in the two legislatures who possessed more than $100,000 in real property represented the low country districts; the two exceptions were Senators J. F. Marshall of Abbeville and J. Duncan Allen of Barnwell.

More than half of the 1860 South Carolina legislators held in excess of $25,000 in personal property,[64] and twenty-six had more than $100,000. Only 14 of the 152 legislators were listed as having no personal property. The median for house members listed with personal property was $26,000; for senate members, $50,000.

Although most legislators who owned large amounts of real property resided in the Tidewater region, slightly more legislators who held in excess of $100,000 in personal property came from the up country area of the state rather than from the Tidewater (fourteen of twenty-six). Most of the wealthier legislators came from the so-called "black" districts or parishes: only two of the twenty-six legislators who held more

[64] Based upon manuscript returns of Schedule No. 1, Free Inhabitants, Eighth Census of United States, 1860. The 1850 census does not report personal property holdings for individuals; hence there is no way of ascertaining this information for members of the thirty-ninth legislature. For an account of property holding of South Carolina legislators at an earlier time, see Jackson Turner Main, "Government by the People: The American Revolution and the Democratization of the Legislatures," *William and Mary Quarterly*, XXIII (July, 1966), 403–404.

TABLE 3

OCCUPATIONS OF MEMBERS OF SOUTHERN LEGISLATURES

| *Legislature* | *Occupation* | *Percentages* 1850 | 1860 |
|---|---|---|---|
| South Carolina | Agriculture | 58.2 | 60.0 |
| | Law | 24.8 | 21.3 |
| | Other | 17.0 | 18.7 |
| Georgia | Agriculture | 64.1 | 65.9 |
| | Law | 17.8 | 18.3 |
| | Other | 18.1 | 15.8 |
| Florida | Agriculture | Not | 68.0 |
| | Law | Determined | 12.0 |
| | Other | | 20.0 |
| Alabama | Agriculture | 58.8 | 57.4 |
| | Law | 26.1 | 22.6 |
| | Other | 15.1 | 20.0 |
| Mississippi | Agriculture | 63.3 | 65.2 |
| | Law | 24.1 | 19.4 |
| | Other | 12.6 | 15.4 |
| Louisiana | Agriculture | 44.4 | 56.3 |
| | Law | 23.4 | 19.9 |
| | Other | 32.2 | 23.8 |
| Texas | Agriculture | 50.0 | 46.0 |
| | Law | 25.0 | 26.6 |
| | Other | 25.0 | 27.4 |

than $100,000 in personal property, Allan Macfarlan of Chesterfield and Robert G. McCaw of York, lived in districts with less than 50 per cent slaves in the total population.[65]

[65] Based upon Eighth Census of United States, vol. I, *Population,* 448–53. See also Schultz, *Nationalism and Sectionalism in South Carolina,* 91, for a listing of districts

Four of every five members in the 1850 and 1860 South Carolina legislatures were listed as slaveholders in Schedule No. 2 of the federal census. That is, 140 members of the thirty-ninth assembly (80.5 per cent) and 143 members of the forty-fourth assembly (81.7 per cent) owned slaves. In both legislatures more than half the members, 53.5 per cent in 1850 and 55.4 per cent in 1860, owned twenty slaves or more and were thus in the "planter" class, if one considers twenty slaves a holding of plantation size.[66] As one might expect from the variations described in property holding, the median holding of slaveowners in the senate was considerably higher in both 1850 and 1860 than in the house. Median for the senate slaveholders was thirty-six slaves in 1850 and fifty-two slaves in 1860, whereas for the lower house it was fourteen slaves in 1850 and sixteen slaves in 1860.

Twenty South Carolina legislators in 1850 and sixteen in 1860 owned one hundred slaves or more. Twenty-three of these "great" planters represented parishes from the low country, while only thirteen came from the districts of the up country. All but two of the thirty-six holders of one hundred slaves or more represented districts with more than 50 per cent slave population; the exceptions were again Senator Robert G. McCaw of York and Representative Allan Macfarlan of Chesterfield. The largest slaveholder in either the thirty-ninth or forty-fourth assembly was Senator Joshua J. Ward, wealthy rice planter from the Georgetown district for whom the 1850

by percentage of slaves in total population. Every one of the thirteen individuals who held more than $100,000 in real property came from "black" districts (those with 50 per cent or more of total population slaves).

66 This is the figure given by Ulrich B. Phillips, *Life and Labor in the Old South* (Boston, 1929), 339.

manuscript census enumerated 1,193 slaves. Other legislators with 500 slaves or more were John L. Manning of Clarendon, who held 648 slaves, many of whom were on his sugar plantation in Louisiana; Plowden Weston, holder of 779 slaves in Prince George's; and John H. Read, holder of 521 slaves, also of Prince George's.

The Georgia legislators were only moderately possessed of real property, and extensive variations existed.[67] Slaveholders were well represented: 122 members, or 69.7 per cent, of the 1850 legislature and 210 members, or 71.6 per cent, of the 1860 legislature were listed in the federal census as slaveholders. Fifty-two of them, or 29.8 per cent, in 1850 and eighty-five, or 29.0 per cent, in 1860 possessed twenty slaves or more and thus properly belong in the planter class. In both legislatures the median number of slaves owned was higher in the senate, thirty in 1850 and seventeen in 1860, than in the house, fifteen in both 1850 and 1860. Individual holdings in the 1850's ranged from one slave each for fifteen different members to one hundred or more slaves owned by each of seven different legislators. Largest individual slaveholders were Randolph Spalding of McIntosh, who had 252 slaves, and L. M. Hill of Wilkes, who had 236.

Legislators in the Gulf states, like those in Georgia, were generally holders of moderate amounts of real property. However, most legislators in those states owned more personal property than did members of the Georgia assembly. Notable in this respect were senators in Florida and Alabama, with medians in personal property in excess of $40,000. Even in

[67] Median property holding, both real and personal, for Georgia house members in 1860 was $13,000; for Georgia senators it was $21,000. This may be compared with the medians for South Carolina: representatives, $36,000, and senators, $75,000.

frontier Texas the legislators had a higher median in personal property than did those in Georgia.[68]

Although the amount of property owned varied greatly from legislator to legislator in the states of the lower South, in all cases the amount of real property held by each increased in the decade 1850–60.[69] In some cases, Alabama for example, the increase was very great; in others, such as Georgia, it was only modest. In all of the states the median of personal property held in 1860 by the legislators was higher than the median for real property. Indeed, the figures showing personal property holdings are quite impressive and indicate that most state legislators in 1860 were men of substantial means.

More than half of these men were slaveholders, too. A comparison of the 1850 and 1860 federal censuses reveals, in fact, an increase in the number of legislators in the slaveowner category,[70] an increase that was particularly noticeable in the states of the Southwest. In Alabama the percentage of slaveholders grew from 66.4 in 1850 to 76.3 in 1860, in Mississippi from 61.5 to 73.4, in Louisiana from 42.6 to 63.8, and in Texas from 38.8

[68] See tables in Appendix I which give a breakdown of property holding for legislators in each of the states of the lower South.

[69] It must be noted, of course, that there are limitations to the use of dollar figures based upon the census returns. Raw dollar values as used in the census do not necessarily indicate real wealth as prices of various items, including slaves, fluctuated during the 1850's. Ulrich B. Phillips, *American Negro Slavery* (Reprint, Gloucester, Mass., 1952), 371, and Lewis C. Gray, *History of Agriculture in the Southern United States to 1860* (Reprint, Gloucester, Mass., 1958), II, 666–67, both point out that the value of slaves rose considerably in the 1850's. Eugene D. Genovese, *The Political Economy of Slavery: Studies in the Economy & Society of the Slave South* (New York, 1965), 69, notes that commodity prices in general were 10 to 16 per cent higher in 1859 than in 1849.

[70] Herbert J. Doherty, Jr., *The Whigs of Florida, 1845–1854* (*University of Florida Monographs, Social Sciences,* No. 1, Winter, 1959; Gainesville, 1959), 68, lists a higher percentage of slaveholders among Whigs and Democrats in the 1845–54 period than was found by this writer in his study of 1860.

TABLE 4

MEDIAN REAL PROPERTY HOLDING OF MEMBERS OF SOUTHERN LEGISLATURES

| *Legislature* | *1850* | *1860* |
|---|---|---|
| South Carolina | House $8,000<br>Senate $11,000 | House $8,000<br>Senate $25,000 |
| Georgia | House $4,000<br>Senate $5,000 | House $4,000<br>Senate $8,000 |
| Florida | Not Determined | House $2,000<br>Senate $10,000 |
| Alabama | House $3,000<br>Senate $3,500 | House $6,000<br>Senate $18,000 |
| Mississippi | House $1,500<br>Senate $3,000 | House $7,000<br>Senate $7,500 |
| Louisiana | House $3,000<br>Senate $8,000 | House $10,000<br>Senate $11,004 |
| Texas | House $2,000<br>Senate $4,154 | House $8,600<br>Senate $10,000 |

to 54.1.[71] Many of these slaveholder-legislators were small operators, but the median holding in each of the states in 1860 was greater than ten slaves.[72] It will be noted, too, that while the percentage of planters in the legislatures increased in each of

[71] In only two of the seven states studied was there an actual increase in the percentage of slaveholders in the total population during the 1850 decade. In each of these, Texas and Mississippi, the percentage of increase was less than 1 per cent.

[72] There was an increase in the median number of slaves held by legislators in most states, but this was not so substantial as the increased percentage of slaveholders present in the legislative bodies. Median holding for slaveholders was highest in South Carolina (sixteen for house members and fifty-two for senators in 1860), but the medians for Alabama and Mississippi legislators were nearly as high.

the states during this period, with the exception of Georgia, in only one legislature—South Carolina—was there a planter majority.

TABLE 5

MEDIAN PERSONAL PROPERTY HOLDING OF MEMBERS OF SOUTHERN LEGISLATURES

| *Legislature* | *1860* |
|---|---|
| South Carolina | House $24,000<br>Senate $45,000 |
| Georgia | House $9,000<br>Senate $13,000 |
| Florida | House $7,000<br>Senate $42,000 |
| Alabama | House $15,000<br>Senate $40,500 |
| Mississippi | House $15,000<br>Senate $20,000 |
| Louisiana | House $8,000<br>Senate $24,835 |
| Texas | House $10,000<br>Senate $15,000 |

The typical legislator who emerges from a composite study of the various states of the lower South in the pre-Civil War decade is thus a middle-aged, southern-born planter or farmer. Quite often the southern lawmaker also had economic interests in law or business and in most instances was a holder of both real and personal property, although the size of individual holdings varied considerably. The typical legislator was also a small slaveholder, but with a tendency for greater holdings in slaves in 1860 than in 1850.

TABLE 6

SLAVEHOLDERS IN SOUTHERN LEGISLATURES

| Legislature | 1850 | 1860 |
|---|---|---|
| *Percentages of Slaveholders* | | |
| South Carolina | 80.5 | 81.7 |
| Georgia | 69.7 | 71.6 |
| Florida | Not Determined | 55.4 |
| Alabama | 66.4 | 76.3 |
| Mississippi | 61.5 | 73.4 |
| Louisiana | 42.6 | 63.8 |
| Texas | 38.8 | 54.1 |
| *Percentages of Planters* | | |
| South Carolina | 53.5 | 55.4 |
| Georgia | 29.8 | 29.0 |
| Florida | Not Determined | 20.0 |
| Alabama | 33.6 | 40.8 |
| Mississippi | 30.3 | 49.5 |
| Louisiana | 19.8 | 23.5 |
| Texas | 5.5 | 18.1 |

## *Rotation in Office*

Turnover in the legislatures was high, a condition still familiar to students of state legislatures. Most southern lawmakers served only briefly in the state capital, retiring from legislative service after one session. In Mississippi, for example, 261 of the

427 individuals who served in the house of representatives during the 1850's, or 61.1 per cent, held office only one term. An additional 133 representatives, or 31.2 per cent, served only two terms during the period.[73] And in Florida four of every five men who served in the house of representatives in the pre-Civil War decade served only one term. Rotation in the Florida senate was even more pronounced; only two men held office more than four years during the period 1846–60. The majority of Florida senators served only one term, and many resigned before their term was complete.[74] In Texas only sixty of the 440 men who served in the lower house of the legislature in the pre-Civil War decade served more than one term. This meant, of course, that the majority of legislators had little influence in formulating governmental policy or doing more than introducing minor or local bills. Real power in the legislatures generally lay in the hands of a few members who, through years of political service, had acquired the mastery of governmental machinery as well as the chairmanships of the more powerful legislative committees.

### *Political Parties, the Legislature, and Legislative Characteristics*

In all the states of the lower South, with the exception of South Carolina on the extreme east and Texas on the extreme west, a strong two-party system existed in the 1840's which

[73] Names of Mississippi legislators for the period are given in Dunbar Rowland, *The Official and Statistical Register of the State of Mississippi* (Madison, 1917), 190–277.

[74] Based upon a close examination of the typewritten list of legislative members in the Florida State Library, Tallahassee.

expressed itself in a Whig-Democrat struggle for control of the state legislatures.[75] Examination of personal characteristics of party members in the 1850 state legislatures has revealed significant differences in property holding between Whigs and Democrats in the Georgia-Alabama-Florida axis and those in the Mississippi-Louisiana area.[76] In Georgia, Florida, and Alabama a higher percentage of Whigs possessed real property and slaves than did Democrats. Also, Whigs had higher median holdings in both real and slave property in these states.[77] In contrast, there was a higher percentage of both real property holders and slaveholders among Democratic legislators in Mississippi and Louisiana, and in both of these states Democratic legislators had a higher median in real property than did

[75] And even in traditionally Democratic Texas the American, or Know Nothing, party made strong inroads in the mid-1850's. More than a dozen members of the party were elected to the state legislature in 1855. See *Texas State Times,* August 11, 18, 1855; *Texas State Gazette,* August 11, 18, 1855; Litha Crews, "The Know Nothing Party in Texas" (M.A. thesis, University of Texas, 1925), 105; and Ralph A. Wooster, "An Analysis of the Texas Know Nothings," *Southwestern Historical Quarterly,* LXX (January, 1967), 415–16.

[76] Various sources were used to determine party membership. Especially important were the Augusta (Ga.) *Chronicle and Sentinel,* October 10, 1849, and October 12, 1859; Columbus (Ga.) *Enquirer,* August 7, 1860; Lewy Dorman, *Party Politics in Alabama From 1850 Through 1860* (Wetumpka, Ala., 1935), 198–214; William Garrett, *Reminiscences of Public Men in Alabama for Thirty Years* (Atlanta, 1872); Thomas A. Owen, *History of Alabama and Dictionary of Alabama Biography* (Chicago, 1921); Vicksburg *Tri-Weekly Whig.* November 17, 28, and December 5, 1849; New Orleans *Bee,* November 22, 1849, and January 21, 1850; and New Orleans *Daily Delta,* December 1, 1849. For Florida a thorough study of state legislators may be found in Doherty's *The Whigs of Florida.*

[77] Median holding in slaves was higher for Whigs in each of the three states. These medians for Whigs were twenty slaves in Georgia, eleven in Florida, and seventeen in Alabama; for Democrats ten in Georgia, seven in Florida, and sixteen in Alabama. Median holding in real property was higher for Whigs in two of the states (Whigs $1,850 in Florida and $3,400 in Alabama; Democrats $800 in Florida and $2,500 in Alabama), and the same for Democrats and Whigs in Georgia ($5,000).

Whigs. The median in slaves held was slightly higher for Whigs than for Democrats in Mississippi, but the reverse was true in Louisiana.[78] These differences in property holdings between Whigs and Democrats were not, however, so great as to provide a real barrier to those wishing to cross party lines. Certainly in respect to legislative members in the late antebellum period, one could not properly claim that the Whigs throughout the lower South were the "broadcloth and silk stocking party."[79]

Differences between Whig and Democratic legislators in respect to age and place of birth varied from state to state. In Georgia and Florida, for example, Whig legislators were on the average older than their Democratic opponents. In Mississippi, Louisiana, and Alabama, Democratic legislators were older than Whig legislators. In Georgia, Florida, and Alabama a higher percentage of Whigs was born in the upper South than were Democrats; in Mississippi and Louisiana the reverse was true—a higher percentage of Democrats was born in the upper South. On the other hand, a higher percentage of Democrats in the Georgia, Florida, and Alabama legislatures was born in the lower South, and a higher percentage of Whigs in the Mississippi and Louisiana legislatures was born in the lower South.

[78] Median for Whig slaveholders in Mississippi was eighteen slaves, compared to seventeen for Democratic legislators; median for Whig slaveholders in Louisiana was twelve slaves, compared to thirteen for Democratic legislators.

[79] For the point of view that southern Whigs were a class party see Arthur C. Cole, *The Whig Party in the South* (Reprint, New York, 1962), 69–73. For a study emphasizing economic similarities of leading Alabama Whigs and Democrats see Thomas B. Alexander, *et al.*, "The Basis of Alabama's Ante-Bellum Two-Party System," *Alabama Review*, XIX (October, 1966), 243–76.

In Georgia, Florida, and Louisiana, more Whigs than Democrats were engaged in agriculture. In Alabama and Missis-

TABLE 7

PROPERTY HOLDING OF POLITICAL FACTIONS IN 1850 SOUTHERN LEGISLATURES

| | *Real Property* | |
|---|---|---|
| *State* | *Percentage of Democrats* | *Percentage of Whigs* |
| Georgia | 87.7 | 89.5 |
| Florida | 63.0 | 79.0 |
| Alabama | 81.2 | 84.9 |
| Mississippi | 88.5 | 83.3 |
| Louisiana * | 77.1 | 66.6 |

| | *Slaveholding* | |
|---|---|---|
| *State* | *Percentage of Democrats* | *Percentage of Whigs* |
| Georgia | 64.2 | 77.0 |
| Florida | 74.0 | 88.0 |
| Alabama | 65.7 | 67.3 |
| Mississippi | 65.7 | 58.8 |
| Louisiana * | 38.8 | 34.0 |

* House members only

sippi, however, more Democrats than Whigs were farmers and planters.[80] In all of the states except Louisiana a higher percentage of lawyers was found among Whigs than among Demo-

[80] These findings are similar to those by Grady McWhiney, "Were the Whigs a Class Party in Alabama?" *Journal of Southern History,* XXIII (November, 1957), 510–22. In this excellent article Professor McWhiney studies personal characteristics of thirty-eight congressmen and more than two hundred legislators from Alabama for the period 1835–56.

crats, and there the percentage was about even.[81] Other occupations were so numerous that no real pattern can be ascertained except for the general tendency of more Democratic legislators than Whigs to have occupations in other than law or agriculture.

Although individual legislators had such diverse backgrounds that one cannot properly support the contention that Whig politicians active in state government at mid-century were a class faction, the county background of legislators indicates that Whig strength in the lower South on the state level was greater in the rich, heavily slave-populated counties. In all seven states, and especially in Georgia, Florida, and Alabama, the so-called black counties elected a larger percentage of Whigs than Democrats to the legislature. Conversely, a larger percentage of Democratic legislators was elected from counties with less than 50 per cent slaves in the total population.[82]

The disintegration of the Whig party in the pre-Civil War decade left state governments more and more in the complete domain of the Democrats. Although some Whigs continued to seek political office under a different name (for example, "Opposition party," "Union party") and others participated in the

[81] Which confirms the contention of Charles G. Sellers, Jr., "Who Were the Southern Whigs?" *American Historical Review,* LIX (January, 1954), 341. This differs from the findings of Thomas B. Alexander, *et al.,* in a study of local Whig and Democratic members for the period. In this study, "Who Were the Alabama Whigs?" *Alabama Review,* XVI (January, 1963), 5–19, Alexander found a slightly higher percentage of lawyers among the Democrats and a higher percentage of farmers and planters among the Whigs.

[82] In the 1850 Alabama legislature, for example, thirty-one Whigs and seventeen Democrats represented the black counties; twenty-seven Whigs and fifty-nine Democrats represented the nonblack counties. In Georgia forty-eight Whig legislators in 1850 represented black counties, while only twenty-two Democrats came from the same areas; forty Democrats and twenty-five Whigs represented nonblack counties.

American, or Know Nothing, movement in the mid-1850's,[83] many simply transferred their allegiance to the Democrats as party issues became subordinate to sectional issues on the eve of the Civil War.[84]

[83] The American party elected a number of state legislators in southern states in 1855–56. In most cases the factions making up this movement were so diverse that the party quickly disintegrated. An exception was in New Orleans, where the party continued to gain legislative victories throughout the 1850's. See Leon Cyprian Soulé, *The Know Nothing Party in New Orleans: A Reappraisal* (Baton Rouge, 1961).

[84] That the principles of the Whig party continued to persist in southern politics long after the disintegration of party organization now seems clear. See especially two articles by Thomas B. Alexander, "Persistent Whiggery in Alabama and the Lower South, 1860–1867," *Alabama Review,* XII (January, 1959), 35–52, and "Persistent Whiggery in the Confederate South, 1860–1877," *Journal of Southern History,* XXVII (August, 1961), 305–29.

☆☆

# THE GOVERNORS

*Social Leaders in Politics*

In his study of constitutional developments in Alabama, Malcolm Cook McMillan notes that the executive article of the 1819 Alabama constitution reflected "the Revolutionary and post-Revolutionary feeling against the Governor."[1] Unpleasant memories of executive authority exercised during the colonial era and even later under territorial government led the Alabama constitution-makers to limit the governor's prerogatives. Although the governor was given the authority to grant pardons and reprieves, to issue proclamations, to make interim appointments, and to command the militia, many of the powers normally associated with the executive were in the hands of the legislature. Appointment of the secretary of state, state treasurer, comptroller of public accounts, and high-ranking militia officers, for example, was reserved for the assembly. The governor was given the power to hold up unfavorable legislation, but his veto was merely suspensive; the legislature could override his veto by a simple majority of both houses.[2]

The position of governor in most of the other states in the lower South was similar to that in Alabama. Whether the state was generally conservative or democratic in terms of suffrage opportunities and restrictions, the governor's office was in most

[1] McMillan, *Constitutional Development in Alabama,* 40. McMillan notes this attitude had been accentuated during the territorial period by controversies between the people and Governor Winthrop Sargent and between the territorial legislature and Governor Robert Williams.

[2] Thorpe, *Federal and State Constitutions,* I, 103–106.

states "a sort of civic crown with which to honor exceptional public men." [3]

In no other state of the region did the governor have fewer powers than in South Carolina. In the Palmetto state the legislature's authority was complete, and the governor was a mere figurehead. Chosen by the legislature for a two-year period, the chief executive in South Carolina could grant pardons and reprieves, remit fines and forfeitures, make recommendations to the assembly, convene the assembly on special occasions, and command the militia; but he had no appointive power, could not veto legislation, and was ineligible for re-election for four years after his term of office.[4]

In neighboring Georgia the governor had slightly more authority than in South Carolina. Here he had at least limited appointive powers and could veto legislative measures. His veto could be overriden only by a two-thirds majority of the legislature. Too, he had a degree of independence from the legislature in that he was popularly elected for a two-year term and could seek re-election.[5]

In three other states, Florida, Mississippi, and Texas, the governor's position was much like that in Georgia. In all three states the governor was popularly elected, had some appointive powers, and could seek re-election.[6] In both Texas and Mississippi the governor served a two-year term but was ineligible to

[3] Wallace, *History of South Carolina,* IV, 351.

[4] Thorpe, *Federal and State Constitutions,* VI, 3261–62.

[5] *Ibid.,* II, 796–98, 805. Originally Georgia governors were selected by the legislature, but a constitutional amendment in 1824 gave this power to the people.

[6] The governor in Texas originally appointed all judges, the secretary of state, and the attorney general; but he lost the power to appoint judges and the attorney general under a constitutional amendment in 1850. For the governor's role in Texas prior to the Civil War see Fred Gantt, Jr., *The Chief Executive in Texas* (Austin, 1964), 15–27.

serve more than four years in any six-year period. In Florida the governor served a four-year term but could not succeed himself. In all three states the governor possessed the veto power. In Florida this could be overridden by a simple majority of both houses; in Mississippi and Texas a two-thirds majority was required.

At one time Louisiana governors had more power than any of the chief executives in the southern states, but by the 1850's they occupied a position similar to that in the other states. Unlike the states in the rest of the lower South where the legislature always dwarfed the executive, Louisiana's first constitution had "envisaged an executive co-ordinate with the legislature"[7] and had given considerable power to the governor. Under the Constitution of 1812 the governor of Louisiana was commander of the armed forces of the state, had the power to veto legislation (which could be overridden by a two-thirds vote), and had widespread appointive authority. Not only did he appoint judges, sheriffs, prosecuting attorneys, and court clerks, he also selected the secretary of state and attorney general of the state. In essence, he controlled most of the administrative structure of Louisiana.[8] The only two officers appointed by the assembly were the state treasurer and printer. Even here, the governor had some power: he could appoint these officers if a vacancy occurred during a legislative recess.

The first Louisiana state constitution provided for an indirect form of electing the governor. The assembly was to choose

[7] James W. Prothro, "A Study of Constitutional Developments in the Office of Governor of Louisiana" (M.A. thesis, Louisiana State University, 1948), 49.

[8] *Ibid.*, 49. See Thorpe, *Federal and State Constitutions,* III, 1384–86, for constitutional provisions relating to the executive.

the chief executive from the two individuals who received the highest number of popular votes. In actual practice this meant that the people chose the governor, however, for not once did the legislature fail to choose the candidate with the highest number of votes. The governor served for four years and was ineligible to succeed himself. An interesting feature of the 1812 constitution was the requirement that the governor of Louisiana visit the different parishes of the state at least once in every two years "to inform himself of the state of the militia and the general condition of the country." [9]

The governor's powers were reduced in Louisiana by both the constitutions of 1845 and 1852. Although the assembly was completely removed from the election process when the people were given full power to elect the governor in 1845, the governor's appointive powers were restricted. The Constitution of 1845 provided that sheriffs, justices of the peace, and clerks of district courts, all formerly appointed by the governor, were now subject to popular election.[10] The governor retained only the right to choose the secretary of state, district attorneys, and the newly created superintendent of public education. In 1852, even these appointive powers were taken from the governor, and the offices were made subject to popular election. Louisiana governors retained the veto power but little else. As one writer has said, "the governor was no longer a chief executive in fact, whatever the Constitution might call him." [11]

[9] Thorpe, *Federal and State Constitutions,* III, 1385.

[10] Prothro, "A Study of Constitutional Developments in the Office of Governor of Louisiana," 57, points out that the governor also lost the right to appoint clerks of the supreme court. Henceforth, they would be appointed by the court itself. See also Ben B. Taylor, Jr., "The Appointive and Removal Powers of the Governor of Louisiana" (M.A. thesis, Louisiana State University, 1935).

[11] Prothro, "A Study of Constitutional Developments in the Office of Governor of Louisiana," 64.

### *Constitutional Requirements*

Constitutional requirements for governor were basically similar throughout the lower South. In all states except Louisiana the minimum age requirement was thirty years. In Louisiana both the constitutions of 1812 and 1845 set an age minimum of thirty-five years, but this was lowered to twenty-eight years by the Constitution of 1852. All states required some form of citizenship, but in some cases this could be state citizenship. In South Carolina, for example, the Constitution of 1790 merely provided that the chief executive "hath resided within this State and been a citizen thereof ten years." [12] In Louisiana the constitutions of 1812 and 1845 required American citizenship, but the 1852 constitution provided merely that the governor be "a citizen and a resident within the State" without specific reference to American citizenship.[13]

The period of citizenship and residence within the state required for chief executives varied. Georgia governors were required to be American citizens for twelve years and residents of the state for six years; South Carolina governors had no residency requirements other than the ten-year state citizenship already mentioned; Mississippi governors had to be citizens of the United States for twenty years and residents of the state for five years; and Florida governors had to be citizens of the United States for ten years or inhabitants of Florida at the time of the adoption of the Constitution of 1838 and residents of the state five years prior to election. Residency requirements

[12] Thorpe, *Federal and State Constitutions,* VI, 3262.

[13] The 1852 constitution specified that a member of the legislature "be a citizen of the United States." *Ibid.,* III, 1412.

for governor in Louisiana changed several times in the antebellum period: the Constitution of 1812 required only six years of residency prior to election; the Constitution of 1845 increased this to fifteen years; and the Constitution of 1852 reduced it to four years. Alabama required only four years of residency for her governors but was unique in stipulating that governors be "native citizens of the United States."[14] Texas, a young state with many immigrants, had the simplest requirements of all: United States citizenship and three-years' state residence.

The older states in the region, South Carolina, Georgia, and Louisiana, and even one newer state, Mississippi, had property qualifications for governor at one time, but by the pre-Civil War decade these had been abolished in all except South Carolina, which continued to require chief executives to possess property valued at "fifteen hundred pounds sterling." In Georgia the governor was originally required to own five hundred acres of land in the state and other property to amount to four thousand dollars, but a constitutional amendment removed this restriction in 1847. In Louisiana the Constitution of 1812 required the governor to own a landed estate valued at five thousand dollars, but this was not included in the constitutions of 1845 and 1852. A requirement that Mississippi governors own six hundred acres of land or real estate valued at two thousand dollars was dropped when that state adopted a new constitution in 1832. Florida, Texas, and Alabama never had property qualifications for the office of governor.

Several states excluded specific groups from serving as gov-

[14] McMillan, *Constitutional Development in Alabama,* 38.

ernor. The reform movement to eliminate dueling was reflected in both Florida and Louisiana, where constitutional restrictions barred duelists from the governorship. Efforts in the Mississippi constitutional convention of 1832 to require an anti-dueling oath for all civil officers were defeated, the constitution simply providing that the legislature was empowered to make such a requirement if it wished. An article from the previous Mississippi constitution excluding all persons from civil office who did not believe in God was retained in the Constitution of 1832.[15] One earlier section barring ministers of the gospel from public office in Mississippi was, however, eliminated in 1832. Florida and Louisiana continued to exclude ministers from the governorship or the legislature. Florida also prohibited bank presidents from serving as governor or legislator.

## *Personal Characteristics and Party Affiliations*

Most of the men who served as governor in the late antebellum period were prominent political and social leaders in their states. The majority of them were born in the South, were planters or lawyers by occupation, and had served in the state legislature or the national Congress. Many of them had had some type of military service prior to their election as governor. While several of the chief executives had rather humble beginnings, most of them owned sizable amounts of property by the time they became governors. The majority of the antebellum governors were slaveholders; in fact, all of those chosen in the prewar decade owned slaves, and two thirds of them

[15] Drake, "Constitutional Development in Mississippi," 158; Thorpe, *Federal and State Constitutions,* IV, 2039–41, 2043–44, 2060–61.

held twenty or more and thus belonged in the planter class.[16]

Nowhere in the lower South did governors occupy a higher social position than in South Carolina. The six men elected as chief executive in the Palmetto state in the 1850's were all well-known social and civic leaders.[17] All were wealthy plantation owners, residing in parishes or districts which had more than 50 per cent slaves in the total population. Five of the six owned more than one hundred slaves, and all of them possessed more than $150,000 in property. One of the South Carolina governors, John L. Manning, was a millionaire and one of the wealthiest men in the South.[18]

Although governors in other states were usually men of means, none could compare with the South Carolinians in social background and wealth. Most of the Georgia governors, for example, were self-made men who had studied law and through hard work and ingenuity had won positions of leadership. All but one of the twenty men who served as governor

[16] Based upon information taken from the manuscript returns of Schedule No. 2, Slave Inhabitants, of the Seventh and Eighth United States Censuses.

[17] Biographical data for South Carolina governors may be found in the *Dictionary of American Biography,* I, 71–72, 223–24; VII, 325; J. Harold Easterby (ed.), *The South Carolina Rice Factor as Revealed in the Papers of Robert F. W. Allston* (Chicago, 1954); and Benjamin F. Perry, *Reminiscences of Public Men* (Philadelphia, 1883), 153–78.

[18] Based upon information taken from manuscript returns of Schedules No. 1 and No. 2 of the Eighth United States Census. John Hugh Means owned 127 slaves and held $27,144 in real and $133,082 in personal property; Manning owned 648 slaves (616 of them in Ascension Parish, Louisiana) and held $1,256,000 in real and $890,000 in personal property; James Hopkins Adams owned 192 slaves and held $80,000 in real and $155,000 in personal property; Robert F. W. Allston owned 631 slaves and held $150,000 in real and $305,000 in personal property; William H. Gist owned 188 slaves and held $80,000 in real and $200,000 in personal property; and Francis W. Pickens owned 82 slaves and held $45,400 in real and $244,206 in personal property.

during the sixty-three years between the adoption of the Constitution of 1798 and the Civil War had legislative experience in either the state assembly or Congress, and many times in both.[19]

The four men who served as chief executive of Georgia during the pre-Civil War decade—George W. Towns, Howell Cobb, Herschel V. Johnson, and Joseph E. Brown—were representative of governors of the state in many ways. All but Brown, a native of South Carolina, were born in Georgia, all had studied law, and although all were slaveholders only Johnson, who owned forty-seven slaves, could be classified as a planter.[20] Cobb and Brown were in their middle thirties when inaugurated, and Towns and Johnson were in their middle forties. Towns had only a limited education, but Johnson and Cobb were graduates of Franklin College, now the University of Georgia, and Brown was a graduate of the Yale Law School. Only Towns and Brown served in the state legislature prior to becoming governor, but Towns, Johnson, and Cobb had served in the United States Congress. Johnson, who was listed with $22,800 in real and $120,000 in personal property in 1860, was wealthiest of the four, but the others held considerable property.[21]

[19] Nine of the Georgia governors were elected for a second consecutive term, and two returned later to serve another term. Albert B. Saye, *Constitutional History of Georgia,* 176–77.

[20] Based on manuscript returns of U.S. Census, 1850 and 1860, Schedule No. 2, Slave Inhabitants, Georgia. Towns owned seven slaves, Cobb eleven slaves, and Brown five slaves in 1850. Towns died prior to 1860; Cobb had nine slaves, and Brown had increased his holding to sixteen slaves by 1860.

[21] The 1850 census enumerator for Baldwin County, Georgia, failed to list property holdings of Governor Towns. Howell Cobb was listed with $25,000 in real property in 1850, but only $8,000 in real and $7,500 in personal property in 1860. Brown had only $5,200 in real property in 1850, but had $20,000 in real and $25,000

Eighteen different individuals served as governor of Mississippi during the forty-four years between statehood and secession.[22] Only two of Mississippi's pre-Civil War chief executives, Gerald C. Brandon and John Isaac Guion (who as president of the senate finished out John A. Quitman's term in 1851), were native-born Mississippians. Four were Virginians, four were South Carolinians, two were Georgians, two were North Carolinians, one was an Alabamian, and one was a Tennessean. Two of the governors, David Holmes, chief executive in 1817–20 and briefly again in 1826, and Quitman, chief executive in 1835–36 and 1850–51, were born in the North—Holmes in Pennsylvania and Quitman in New York.[23]

Median age for Mississippi governors when first elected to office was forty-four years.[24] Five governors were in their thirties, six in their forties, three in their fifties, and two in their sixties. Ages ranged from the thirty-one years for Albert Gallatin Brown, governor in 1844–48, to sixty years for William McWillie, governor in 1857–59.

All but five of the prewar governors were lawyers. Several

in personal property in 1860. Biographical data taken from manuscript returns of Seventh and Eighth United States Censuses, 1850 and 1860; *Biographical Directory of American Congress,* 610, 711, 1125–26, 1723; *Dictionary of American Biography,* III, 141–43; VI, 241–44; X, 102–103; XVIII, 615; and Stephen F. Miller, *The Bench and Bar of Georgia* (Philadelphia, 1858), II, 318–41.

[22] Ten of the eighteen held office only one term or less; the eight others served two terms or one full term and part of another. On seven occasions during the period the governor failed to complete his term of office, five simply resigning and two, Walter Leake in 1825 and Abram M. Scott in 1833, dying in office. Rowland, *Official and Statistical Register,* 165–66, 278–79.

[23] Biographical information for Mississippi governors is based largely upon Rowland, *Official and Statistical Register,* 280–306.

[24] This does not include the ages of Guion and James Whitfield, who served only briefly and were not elected. Too, ages figured for Brandon, Quitman, John J. Pettus, and Charles Lynch are those when actually elected; all four had earlier served parts of terms when governors had died or resigned.

were also engaged in planting, and at least one, James Whitfield, had extensive mercantile interests. Sixteen of the governors had served in the territorial or state legislature, eight had previous military experience, seven had been judges, six had served in the federal Congress, five had been delegates to the 1817 constitutional convention, and two had been in the 1832 convention. All the elected governors were or had been Democrats, although George Poindexter, an early Virginia Jeffersonian, became a leader of Mississippi Whigs, and John I. Guion, who served less than a year as the chief executive, was a prominent Whig legislator.

Geographically, the majority of the Mississippi prewar governors came from the rich Delta counties of the southwestern part of the state. Twelve came from this area, one from central Mississippi, one from northern Mississippi, and four from eastern Mississippi. All but three were residents of counties which on the eve of the Civil War had 50 per cent or more slaves in the total population, and eleven of these lived in counties with better than 70 per cent slaves. All but four were from the big cotton-producing counties of the state, i.e., those counties producing twenty thousand bales of cotton annually.[25]

In neighboring Alabama sixteen individuals served as governor during the forty-two years of statehood prior to the Civil War. The first governor, William W. Bibb, died after serving only eight months; and his term was filled by his brother, Thomas, who was president of the state senate and, under the constitution, successor to the governor. Two other Alabama governors, Gabriel Moore and Clement Clay, were elected to the United States Senate and resigned before completing their

[25] Based upon Eighth Census of United States, 1860, vol. I, *Population,* 270, and vol. III, *Agriculture,* 84–85.

tenure as governor, thus leaving the president of the state senate to serve for them. The rest of the governors, except Joshua Martin (1845–47) and Reuben Chapman (1847–49), were elected to and served a second term as chief executive of the state.[26]

Nearly all of the antebellum Alabama governors were southern-born, had some form of legal training, and were holders of slaves and real property. Most of them had gained legislative experience in the state assembly, several had served as judges, and all were members of the Democratic party. The last three governors of the antebellum period, Henry W. Collier, John A. Winston, and Andrew B. Moore, seem typical of the group. All were southerners, all had legislative experience, and all were holders of thirty or more slaves.[27]

The early governors of Louisiana were Whigs, but from 1842, when the first Democratic governor was chosen, until after the Civil War, all the governors were Democrats. Two of the last six, Alexander Mouton and Paul Octave Hébert, were Acadians; two, Isaac Johnson and Robert C. Wickliffe, were lawyers; and all were members of the social aristocracy. Although only one, Mouton, owned more than one hundred slaves, all but one, Wickliffe, owned more than forty.[28]

[26] Garrett, *Reminiscences of Public Men in Alabama,* 774; Owen, *History of Alabama and Dictionary of Alabama Biography,* I, 663–64; and Willis Brewer, *Alabama: Her History, Resources, War Record and Public Men* (Montgomery, 1872), 38–61.

[27] Collier was listed in the 1850 census with eighty-eight slaves and $15,000 in real property, and Winston was listed in the 1860 census with seventy-two slaves and $112,000 in total property. The writer was unable to find an enumeration for Moore in Schedule No. 1 of the 1860 census; he was listed with thirty-three slaves in the slave schedule.

[28] Although most writers refer to Robert C. Wickliffe as a member of the aristocracy, the 1850 census lists him with only $2,100 in real property and five

In Florida the five men who were governors of the state before the Civil War were all residents of the great plantation counties of Middle Florida, and only one, Democrat James E. Broome, was not a planter. In addition, four were Democrats, the exception being Whig Thomas Brown, a conservative Tallahassee planter and hotel man, elected in 1849.[29]

Governors of Texas, youngest of the slaveholding states, were men of property and social standing but could not match the personal wealth of governors in the older states. The six prewar Texas governors were slaveholders, but only one, George T. Wood, owned a large plantation. All but one of the governors, Connecticut-born Elisha M. Pease, were born in the South, and even he had lived in Texas long enough to be considered an "old Texan." All of the governors but one had seen military service of some type. In age they ranged from Hardin R. Runnels, who was only thirty-seven at the time of his election, to the hero of San Jacinto, Sam Houston, who was sixty-six when chosen governor. Only two of the governors had much formal education, but all had been educated in the school of experience. With the exception of Peter H. Bell, all of them had legislative experience prior to becoming governor; and three had prior executive service. By personal charac-

---

slaves. In the 1860 returns for West Feliciana Parish, Wickliffe is reported to have had $1,000 in real property, $1,500 in personal property, and no slaves. Thomas O. Moore, who held 226 slaves and $320,000 in real and $24,300 in personal property, was wealthiest of the Louisiana governors.

[29] Data on Florida governors may be found in Doherty, *The Whigs of Florida*, 26; Williams, "Florida in the Union," 103; William T. Cash, *History of the Democratic Party in Florida* (Tallahassee, 1936), 36–37; Kathryn A. Hanna, *Florida, Land of Change* (Chapel Hill, 1948), 242–43; and Daisy Parker, "John Milton, Governor of Florida," *Florida Historical Quarterly*, XX (April, 1942), 348–61.

teristics and practical experience, all six were leaders qualified to serve as chief executive of the state.[30]

## *Other Executive Officers*

Only three of the states in the lower South, South Carolina, Louisiana, and Texas, had a lieutenant governor in the pre-Civil War decade; and in each of these three states he was elected in the same manner and served the same length of term as the governor. In the other four states the constitutions provided that the president of the senate would exercise the powers of chief executive in the case of the death, resignation, or disability of the governor. In Mississippi there had been a lieutenant governor, but the office was dropped in the Constitution of 1832, "probably for reasons of economy." [31]

Various other executive offices existed in the governmental machinery of the states of the lower South; and in South Carolina, of course, the legislature chose all who filled them. In Florida, Georgia, and Alabama, where the people elected the governor, the legislature chose the secretary of state, treasurer, attorney general, and other executive officers.[32] These executive officers were originally appointed by the governor in Louisiana; but by 1852 the secretary of state, attorney general,

[30] Biographical sketches of Texas governors are found in Walter P. Webb (ed.), *The Handbook of Texas* (Austin, 1952); *Biographical Directory of the Texan Conventions and Congresses, 1832–1845* (Huntsville, 1942); James T. DeShields, *They Sat in High Places* (San Antonio, 1940); and L. E. Daniell, *Personnel of the Texas State Government with Sketches of Representative Men of Texas* (San Antonio, 1892). There are a number of full-length biographies of Houston; superior is Llerena B. Friend's *Sam Houston, The Great Designer* (Austin, 1954).

[31] Drake, "Mississippi Constitutional Convention of 1832," 365.

[32] Florida and Alabama both had a comptroller of public accounts. Georgia had a surveyor-general.

superintendent of public education, and members of the newly created board of public works were all chosen by voters of the state. In Texas and Mississippi, two of the more democratic states in the South, most of the executives (secretary of state, treasurer, attorney general, and auditor of public accounts in Mississippi; attorney general, commissioner of land office, treasurer, and comptroller in Texas) were elected by the people for a two-year term of office.[33] The governor of Texas retained the right to appoint the secretary of state throughout the pre-Civil War years.

As was the case with legislators and governors, rotation of personnel was common among other executive posts. In Mississippi, only three of the fifteen people who served as secretary of state in the antebellum period held office for more than one term. Only one of these three, John A. Grimball, who served twelve years, held office more than two terms. Rotation in office was not quite so high in the post of treasurer, five of sixteen Mississippians holding office in the antebellum period for more than two years. The turnover in personnel was even less in the office of auditor of public accounts in Mississippi; of the eleven men who held office in a forty-four-year period all but one served more than one term.[34] In Texas, too, there was greater continuity in the treasurer's and comptroller's offices; two men served as treasurer and two as comptroller in the fifteen-year period between statehood and secession. On the other hand, seven Texans served as lieutenant governor, seven

[33] Although the treasurer and comptroller were chosen by the legislature in Texas prior to 1850.

[34] Based upon study of names of these officers given in Rowland, *Official and Statistical Register,* 169–72. Duties of these executive officers are listed in *Revised Code of the Statute Laws of the State of Mississippi* (Jackson, 1857), 104–13.

as secretary of state, nine as attorney general, and five as commissioner of the land office during the same period.[35] In Alabama eight men served as secretary of state, seven as treasurer, and five as comptroller during the forty-two years between statehood and secession.[36]

[35] Based upon a study of the manuscript "Register State, County Officers, 1846 to 1854," and the manuscript "Election Register, 1854–1861," in the Texas State Archives, Austin, Texas.

[36] William Garrett, himself secretary of state in Alabama from 1840–52, lists various executive officers in his *Reminiscences of Public Men in Alabama for Thirty Years,* 774–75.

☆☆☆

# COURTS AND JUDGES

## *Development of Judicial Systems*

JUDICIAL SYSTEMS were developed rather slowly and haphazardly in the states of the lower South. The judicial sections of the early constitutions adopted in South Carolina and Georgia, oldest states in the area, were short and contained only brief references to courts and judges.[1] Although constitutions of the newer states provided more elaboration, they too left judicial details to statutory enactment.[2] As a result, most states in the lower South did not have a fully developed court system embracing lower, circuit, and appeals courts until the middle of the nineteenth century.

### *The Lower Courts*

In the older areas of the South the early courts developed along the patterns established during the Colonial era. In both South Carolina and Georgia justices of the peace handled petty cases in Colonial days and continued to do so after independence. In South Carolina the circuit courts, sitting in seven judicial districts, tried most other cases prior to 1785 when a county court system was introduced. In that year, largely through the efforts of Henry Pendleton, a Virginian, the old judicial districts were divided into thirty-four counties with provision made for a court session every three months in each

[1] Green, *Constitutional Development*, 91, notes that "the first state constitutions said very little about the judiciary."

[2] For the early constitutions of South Carolina and Georgia see Thorpe, *Federal and State Constitutions*, II, 777–90; VI, 3241–57.

county. The courts were presided over in each county by seven justices of the peace who were chosen by the legislature and served without pay.[3]

The experience with county courts was not a success in South Carolina. In the coastal area frequent courts were unnecessary as the plantations took care of minor matters themselves; in the Piedmont it was difficult to find seven men in each county who were sufficiently versed in law to serve as justices. After an experiment of some fourteen years the county court system was abolished, and twenty-five judicial districts were created incorporating all the counties. The number of circuit judges, who by an act of 1789 had been given more original and final jurisdiction, was increased from four to six, and they were required to hold court in each of the twenty-five districts.[4]

As in South Carolina, each Georgia county had a number of justices of the peace who handled civil cases not exceeding thirty dollars in value. Originally the Georgia justices of the peace were nominated by the inferior court (a higher local court), were commissioned by the governor, and served for good behavior; but in 1812 they became elective officers chosen by the voters for four-year terms of office.[5] Two such justices

[3] Schaper, "Sectionalism and Representation," 382; and Andrews, *Administrative County Government in South Carolina,* 16.

[4] Schaper, "Sectionalism and Representation," 328. Andrews, *Administrative County Government in South Carolina,* 16–18, points out that in Beaufort, Charleston, and Georgetown the county court system was never placed in effect. He also notes that in some instances after 1798 the judicial and election districts were identical but in many cases they were not. Charleston judicial district, for example, contained ten election districts, while All Saints' election district was partly in the judicial district of Georgetown and partly in that of Horry. In other instances the judicial and election districts were identical except in name.

[5] Thorpe, *Federal and State Constitutions,* II, 799, 802–803.

were chosen in each militia district. Most counties had at least four districts and thus were entitled to eight justices. The number of such districts was increased frequently in the nineteenth century. By the 1850's many counties had six or eight districts, or twelve to sixteen justices. One county, Habersham, had sixteen districts, or thirty-two justices, in 1853.[6]

The most important local governmental body in Georgia was the five-man inferior court. Created in 1789 as a court of limited jurisdiction, the inferior court was made a fundamental tribunal by the Constitution of 1798. Originally the justices were appointed by the assembly, commissioned by the governor, and held office for good behavior as long as they resided in the county, but in 1812 they became elected officers.[7] The inferior court exercised legislative and administrative as well as judicial powers and performed functions comparable to the county court in the upper South. Jurisdiction of the court included all civil cases except those involving land titles.

The Georgia inferior court originally acted also as a court of the ordinary, having jurisdiction over probation of wills, granting letters of administration for settlement of estates, and appointing guardians. Throughout the early nineteenth century the court appointed its own clerk, called "clerk of the court of the ordinary," who acted as a register of probates. In 1852 a new office, the ordinary, was created, and Georgia

[6] Based upon examination of microfilm copy of "Georgia Executive Department, Commission Book, Justices of the Peace, 1853–1861," in Georgia Department of Archives and History, Atlanta.

[7] Thorpe, *Federal and State Constitutions,* II, 802–803. The actual method of election was simplified by further amendment in 1819. See *ibid.,* 804–805, and T. R. R. Cobb, *A Digest of the Statute Laws of Georgia . . . to 1851* (Athens, 1851), 206–207.

inferior judges no longer concerned themselves with this matter.[8]

The lower court systems in the Gulf states were basically similar. In all of them popularly elected justices of the peace handled petty civil cases.[9] In four of these states the justices served two-year terms; in one, Alabama, their tenure was three years. As was the case in Georgia the number of justices of the peace per county was steadily increasing in the nineteenth century, especially in Alabama. Thus Autauga County, Alabama, had eighteen justices of the peace in 1850, Barbour County had twenty-eight, Chambers County had thirty, and Jackson County had fifty.[10] As the majority of justices in the lower South served no more than one term in office, this meant that literally hundreds of southerners briefly held the post of justice of the peace. In forty-one Texas counties, for example, 1,390 individuals served as justices of the peace in the period 1854–61. Of this number only 172 (12.4 per cent) held office for more than one term.[11] In Florida only 173 of the 1,499 individuals who served as justices of the peace in the prewar decade, or 12.3 per cent, held office longer than two years.[12] This rapid

[8] Horatio Marbury and William H. Crawford, *Digest of the Laws of the State of Georgia from Its Settlement as a British Province . . .* (Savannah, 1802), 219; Melvin C. Hughes, *County Government in Georgia* (Athens, 1944), 17; and Warren Grice, "The Old Inferior Court," *Georgia Bar Journal,* VI (August, 1942), 5–14.

[9] In some states the justices of the peace were limited to cases not exceeding $50; in others they were limited to cases not exceeding $100.

[10] Names of justices of the peace are given in the manuscript "Civil Register of County Officials, 1844–1867," vol. III, in the Department of Archives and History, Montgomery, Ala.

[11] Based on "Election Register, 1854–1861," in Texas State Archives, Austin.

[12] Based upon analysis of "Roster of State and County Officers Commissioned by the Governor of Florida, 1845–1868," in the Florida State Library, Tallahassee.

turnover in personnel meant, of course, that more individuals were given the opportunity to serve in public office, but at the same time it meant that most justices were inexperienced and untrained in the functions of their office.

Unlike their counterparts in Georgia and some states of the upper South, county administrative units in the Gulf states performed few judicial functions in the late antebellum period. Although this body still carried the word "court" as part of its title in one state, Texas, and the word "jury" in another, Louisiana, its judicial role diminished in the nineteenth century. In most states a county judge, known by various titles, handled county judicial affairs. Thus in Alabama the probate judge, an officer established in 1850, was charged with performing "all duties now performed by judges of county courts." As a probate judge he had original jurisdiction in probating wills and testaments, appointing guardians of orphans, minors, or those of unsound mind, binding out of apprentices, and settlement and allowances for executors, administrators, and guardians.[13]

In Mississippi a similar court of probate existed in each county. Here the county judge had jurisdiction in probating wills, granting letters testamentary, appointing guardians for minors and lunatics, and examining and approving accounts of executors, administrators, and guardians. Too, probate judges in Mississippi could sit as a court of inquiry in criminal matters and take proper recognizances of parties and their sureties for their appearance at the circuit court.[14] In this

[13] *Acts of the Second Biennial Session of the General Assembly of Alabama . . .* (Montgomery, 1850), 26–27.

[14] *Revised Code of the Statute Laws of the State of Mississippi,* 423–26. Analysis of individual characteristics for sixty-one probate judges listed in the manuscript census

respect the role of the Mississippi county judge was similar to that of the parish judge in Louisiana, the probate judge in Florida, and the chief justice in Texas.

In Alabama, Florida, and Texas the county judge continued to serve on the county administrative board as the presiding officer, either as a voting or ex officio member, throughout the antebellum period.[15] In two other states, Mississippi and Louisiana, the county or parish judge at one time served on the county administrative board but by the 1840's no longer did so.[16] In Texas and Mississippi the county judge was elected by the people as early as the 1830's; in Alabama he became a popularly elected officer in 1850. In two other states, Louisiana and Florida, the judge continued to be appointed by the governor for a four-year term of office.[17]

As was the case for justices of the peace, county judges were ordinarily not experienced or trained in the law. In part this was due to rotation in office, which prevented an individual from gaining valuable experience through years of service,[18]

---

returns shows little difference between state legislators and probate judges in Mississippi. Median age for the judges was forty-two years; thirty-three were born in the lower South, eleven in the upper South, and seven in the northern states. Twenty-four judges listed their occupation as farmer, twelve as lawyer, three as merchant, one as editor, one as clerk, and one as minister. Median real property holding was $3,000; median personal property holding, $5,000. Half of the judges, thirty-one, were slaveholders, but only seven owned twenty or more slaves.

[15] Thompson, *Manual or Digest of Statute Law of Florida,* 57–58, 126–27; *Acts of the Second Biennial Session of the General Assembly of Alabama,* 24–36; Gammel, *The Laws of Texas,* II, 1506–12, 1390–91; III, 44–45, 84, 474.

[16] U. B. Phillips, *The Revised Statutes of Louisiana* (New Orleans, 1856), 406–14; Drake, "Constitutional Development in Mississippi," 152.

[17] Thorpe, *Federal and State Constitutions,* IV, 2056; Thompson, *Manual or Digest of Statute Law of Florida,* 57–58; and Garrett, *Reminiscences of Public Men in Alabama,* 519–20.

[18] For example, 215 of 294 chief justices chosen in Texas, 1854–61, or 73.5 per cent, served only one two-year term. Fifty-nine served two terms, thirteen served

and in part to their occupational backgrounds which were more often in agriculture than in the law.[19]

### *Circuit and Appeals Courts*

By the middle of the nineteenth century all of the states in the lower South had some form of circuit and appeals courts, although the names and roles of the courts varied from state to state. As noted above, South Carolina relied upon circuit judges, who sat in judicial districts throughout the state, to handle both state and county judicial matters. Efforts to establish a separate appeals court in South Carolina were unsuccessful until 1824. In that year a court of appeals was created with full powers in all appeals in law or equity.[20] The experiment was short-lived, however, because the new court offended the nullifiers in the 1830's by annulling the test oath; consequently, the appeals court was abolished in 1835. Its judges were transferred to the law and equity branches, and temporarily the united judges served as a court of appeals for cases of both law and equity. In 1838 two courts of appeal, one in law and one in equity, were created, composed of all the circuit law or equity judges, respectively. Above these was a court of errors, composed of the two appeals groups combined, to which constitutional questions could be referred. In 1859 a

---

three terms, and six served four terms during the period. Based on the manuscript "Election Register, 1854–1861," in Texas State Archives, Austin.

[19] In Mississippi and Texas only one county judge of every four studied listed his occupation as law. Approximately half listed their occupation as agriculture. Based upon information from manuscript returns of Seventh and Eighth United States Censuses, 1850 and 1860.

[20] Until 1868 equity was administered in South Carolina by special judges. Prior to 1784 the governor and council handled these matters; but in that year equity judges were provided for, elected, and made removable by the legislature. In 1808 an equity appeals court was created. Wallace, *History of South Carolina,* II, 460.

new court of appeals, composed of only three judges headed by Chief Justice John Belton O'Neall, was established. Its powers were somewhat curtailed, because the court of errors, made up of all law and equity judges and the appeal judges, was retained as a check on the smaller court of appeals.[21] Throughout the period the South Carolina legislature continued to elect judges to the various courts of the state, thus assuring a measure of legislative control over the judiciary similar to that exercised over the executive branch.

In Georgia supreme and district court judges were also chosen by the legislature. The Constitution of 1798, basic document of government for Georgia in the antebellum period, provided for a superior court and such inferior courts as the legislature might establish. The term "superior" is somewhat misleading as there were at the time three judicial districts, each with a court of final jurisdiction, and this practice was continued. The number of such courts was soon increased to ten, each holding jurisdiction in its district with no supreme court to review decisions. To these courts the constitution gave exclusive jurisdiction in all criminal and land-title cases and appellate jurisdiction in others. The constitution provided that the judges of these courts were to be elected for three-year terms, and as the assembly had elected them in the past this practice was continued.[22]

[21] *Statutes at Large of South Carolina, 1682–1866* (Columbia, 1836–75), XII, 647–48; Wallace, *History of South Carolina,* II, 461. See also O'Neall, *Biographical Sketches of the Bench and Bar of South Carolina,* I, ix–xiii, for a sketch of the early history of the South Carolina judiciary.

[22] Saye, *Constitutional History of Georgia,* 798: George White, *Statistics of the State of Georgia . . .* (Savannah, 1849), 61. In 1835 a constitutional amendment changed the term of office to four years. Miller, *The Bench and Bar of Georgia,* II, 368–78, lists names of superior judges, 1790–1857.

A supreme court was not established in Georgia until 1845. Unfortunate experiences with the United States Supreme Court in the Chisholm and Indian land cases and the expensive delays associated with such courts caused Georgians to look at the establishment of new courts with suspicion. Judges and lawyers, however, continued to feel the need of a supreme court of appeals; and in 1835 a constitutional amendment was ratified, providing for a supreme court of three judges elected by the legislature for such term of office as it might prescribe. The court had no original jurisdiction but was an appellate tribunal for the correction of errors in law and equity in the superior courts. Despite the adoption of the constitutional amendment, there continued to be opposition to the creation of such a court; and it was not until December 10, 1845, that the supreme court was actually established. The act provided that the first judges chosen would serve six-, four-, and two-year terms, but that in the future all judges should serve six-year terms.[23]

Throughout the late antebellum period there were continued demands that Georgia supreme and superior judges be chosen by the people rather than the legislature, but such changes were not forthcoming.[24] Only in regard to judges of the inferior courts and justices of the peace, both made elective

[23] Cobb, *Digest of Statute Laws of Georgia,* 447–53. Fletcher M. Green in his *Constitutional Development of the South Atlantic States,* 258–59, points out that dissatisfaction with a decision of the superior court of the northern circuit of Georgia in 1841, concerning the swearing of witnesses, aroused a storm of protest and contributed to the demand for a court of final resort. See also Bond Almand, "The Supreme Court of Georgia: An Account of Its Delayed Birth," *Georgia Bar Journal,* VI (November, 1943), 95–110, and Ware, *A Constitutional History of Georgia,* 98–106.

[24] Green, *Constitutional Development,* 260.

by constitutional amendment in 1812, were concessions of this type made.

As in South Carolina and Georgia, state judges in Alabama were appointed by the legislature throughout most of the antebellum period. The Alabama Constitution of 1819, basically a liberal document in respect to voting and officeholding, was conservative in respect to the judiciary; judges were elected by joint vote of both houses of the assembly and were given terms of good behavior.[25] Agitation for amending the judiciary article of the constitution began almost the moment the constitutional convention adjourned, but only limited changes were actually made. The life tenure of the judges attracted immediate opposition, and an attempt to limit their terms to four years was introduced and debated in the state senate in 1819 but failed to pass.[26] The opposition continued to mount, however, and was increased by an unpopular decision of the state supreme court in 1827. In 1828 the people of Alabama voted to limit the judges to a seven-year term, but so much confusion occurred in the balloting that the legislature refused to ratify the proposed amendment. The following year the legislature submitted to the people a new amendment to limit judges to a six-year term. This amendment was approved in the late summer, was quickly ratified by the legislature, and became effective in 1830.[27]

The demand for the popular election of judges began soon after the limitation of tenure was approved. The spirit of Jacksonianism was particularly strong in Alabama, and the fact that the neighboring state of Mississippi made provision

[25] Thorpe, *Federal and State Constitutions,* I, 107.

[26] McMillan, *Constitutional Development in Alabama,* 47.

[27] *Ibid.,* 49–51; Thorpe, *Federal and State Constitutions,* I, 114–15.

for popular election of all judges strengthened the cause of those advocating change. In August, 1843, an amendment providing for popular election of county judges was submitted to the voters but was defeated. Six years later the proposal, along with one providing for popular election of circuit court judges as well, was resubmitted, and both were overwhelmingly approved. Thus, in 1850 the first elections for county and circuit judges in Alabama were held.[28]

Alabama supreme court judges and judges of the chancery court, established in 1839, continued to be chosen by the legislature until after the Civil War.[29] Originally the supreme court consisted of judges of the circuit courts sitting collectively as the high tribunal, but in 1832 an act of the legislature provided for a separate and distinct body. From then until 1852 the supreme court was comprised of three justices. In that year the number was increased to five. Two years later it was reduced to three again, the number serving on the eve of the Civil War.[30]

State judges in Florida, Louisiana, and Texas became popularly elected officials in the 1850's. Under the Florida Constitution of 1838 the legislature named all state judges for a term of

[28] McMillan, *Constitutional Development in Alabama,* 64–67; Garrett, *Reminiscences of Public Men in Alabama,* 520; *Acts of the Second Biennial Session of the General Assembly of Alabama,* 37–40; and Thorpe, *Federal and State Constitutions,* I, 116.

[29] The Alabama Constitution of 1865 left the election of supreme court judges and chancellors with the legislature, but the Constitution of 1867 provided that these officers would be elected by the people. Thorpe, *Federal and State Constitutions,* I, 129, 143.

[30] Brewer, *Alabama: Her History, Resources, War Record and Public Men,* 93; *Acts of the Third Biennial Session of the General Assembly of Alabama . . . November, 1851* (Montgomery, 1852), 28.

good behavior, but this was amended in 1853 to provide for popular election for terms of six years.[31] In Louisiana and Texas, state judges originally were appointed by the governor, but they too became popularly elected officers as a result of constitutional changes in the 1850's.

The Louisiana constitutions of 1845 and 1852 made several changes in that state's judiciary. The Constitution of 1812 had created a supreme court of from three to five members, all of whom were appointed by the governor for good behavior. This was changed in 1845 to one chief justice and three associates, all serving for eight years. In 1852 another change provided for four associates rather than three, and for a ten-year elective term of office rather than the eight-year appointive one. Under the new constitution the chief justice was elected by all the qualified voters of the state, while the associates were chosen by voters in one of four newly created election districts.[32]

Up until 1852 Louisiana district court judges, like members of the supreme court, were appointed by the governor. In that year their offices were also made elective and their terms of office reduced from six years to four. There were eighteen such districts in the late 1850's; but one of them, New Orleans, was further subdivided into six districts, each with an elected judge. Under Louisiana law these courts had original jurisdiction in all criminal cases and in all civil cases where the amount of money involved exceeded fifty dollars. Their juris-

[31] Williams, "Florida in the Union," 60. Until 1851 the four circuit judges of Florida served as the supreme court of the state, but in that year a legislative enactment created a separate and distinct body, the Supreme Court of Florida.

[32] Thorpe, *Federal and State Constitutions,* III, 1386–87, 1400–1401, 1418–19.

diction in civil cases thus overlapped that of justices of the peace, who were empowered to handle all civil cases in which less than one hundred dollars was involved.[33]

In Texas, too, constitutional changes in the 1840's and 1850's affected the state's courts. The Constitution of 1836 provided that members of the supreme court, all but one of whom were also district judges, were to be appointed for a four-year term by the legislature. This situation was altered by the Constitution of 1845, which provided for a three-man body, one chief justice and two associates, who had no other judicial duties and who were appointed by the governor for six years.[34] In 1850 a constitutional amendment made judges of the supreme court, as well as of all other courts in Texas, elective officials.[35]

Judges of Texas district courts were chosen in the same manner as supreme court justices and exercised original jurisdiction in all criminal cases and all civil cases involving sums of one hundred dollars or more. The Constitution of 1845 placed no limitation on the number of such courts, and as the needs of the state grew so did the district judiciary. Rarely did a session of the legislature pass in the pre-Civil War decade without the establishment of a new district court. There were twelve in 1850, sixteen by 1855, and twenty by 1860.[36]

No state in the antebellum South had a more democratic judicial system than Mississippi. As Winbourne Drake points

[33] Phillips, *Revised Statutes of Louisiana,* 280–81, 286–88, 299–307.

[34] J. H. Davenport, *The History of the Supreme Court of the State of Texas* (Austin, 1917), 28–29, and John C. Townes, "Development of the Texas Judicial System," *Quarterly of the Texas State Historical Association,* II (July, 1898), 29–53, 134–51.

[35] See Leila Clark Wynn, "A History of the Civil Courts in Texas," *Southwestern Historical Quarterly,* LX (July, 1956), 4.

[36] Gammel, *The Laws of Texas,* IV, 1378–79.

out in his study of constitutional developments in the state, the constitutional convention of 1832 "made more changes in the judicial article than in any other part of the old constitution and devoted more time to this subject than to any other."[37] As finally adopted the Mississippi Constitution of 1832 made all judicial positions, from the very highest court to the lowest, elective and set definite terms for judges. At the top of the judicial system was the newly created High Court of Errors and Appeals consisting of three judges, one elected by the people in each of three districts and chosen for a six-year term. This court, which had no original jurisdiction, replaced the old supreme court created in 1817.[38]

Mississippi was further divided into a number of circuit court districts consisting of from three to twelve counties each. In each district voters elected a circuit judge who served a four-year term. The circuit court was required to sit at least twice a year in each county and had original jurisdiction in all criminal cases and in all civil cases where the sum in controversy exceeded fifty dollars. A separate superior court of chancery with jurisdiction in matters of equity existed until 1856 when a constitutional amendment transferred equity cases to the circuit courts.[39]

[37] Drake, "Mississippi Constitutional Convention of 1832," 363.

[38] Thorpe, *Federal and State Constitutions,* IV, 2055–57, contains the judicial section of the 1832 constitution. See also Dunbar Rowland, *Courts, Judges, and Lawyers of Mississippi, 1798–1935* (Jackson, 1935), 78–79; James D. Lynch, *The Bench and Bar of Mississippi* (New York, 1881), 187–89; and John F. H. Claiborne, *Mississippi, as a Province, Territory, and State, with Biographical Notices of Eminent Citizens* (Jackson, 1880), 467–75.

[39] Thorpe, *Federal and State Constitutions,* IV, 2056–57, 2065; Lynch, *Bench and Bar of Mississippi,* 534–35; Drake, "Constitutional Development in Mississippi," 217–22; and Rowland, *Official and Statistical Register,* 339. Rowland, 176–83, gives a full list of circuit court judges and chancellors of Mississippi for the period. In 1832

The judges who served on the state courts in the late antebellum lower South generally occupied higher positions in the socio-economic structure of the region than did county judges and justices of the peace. The seven men who served on the Georgia supreme court in the antebellum period, for example, were all respected leaders of their state, slaveholders, and owners of considerable amounts of real property. One, Charles J. McDonald, was a former governor of the state; three, Joseph Henry Lumpkin, Hiram Warner, and Eugenius A. Nisbet, were veteran legislators; one, Henry L. Benning, was a longtime leader in the state Democratic party; and another, Linton Stephens, was one of the wealthiest planters in the state.[40] Six of the thirteen judges who sat on the Alabama supreme court in the prewar decade were former state legislators; two of them, Lyman Gibbons and Edmund S. Dargan, were later members of the secession convention; and two others, William P. Chilton and Richard W. Walker, participated in the Montgomery Convention which created the Confederate States of America. All of the Alabama supreme court justices were substantial property holders, and several maintained extensive planting interests in addition to their law practices.[41]

---

Mississippi was divided into four circuits; these were soon increased to six, and in the 1840's the number rose to ten. For the various district divisions see *Revised Code of the Statute Laws of the State of Mississippi,* 474–79.

[40] In 1860 Linton Stephens held $148,000 in property and owned 113 slaves. Personal data taken from manuscript returns of Seventh and Eighth United States Censuses, 1850 and 1860; Miller, *Bench and Bar of Georgia,* II, 378; Bond Almand, "History of the Supreme Court of Georgia, the First Hundred Years: Part One—January 1, 1846, to June 30, 1858," *Georgia Bar Journal,* VI (February, 1944), 177–206; Charles J. Hilkey, "History of the Supreme Court of Georgia: Part Two—July 1, 1858, to December 31, 1870," *ibid.,* VI (May, 1944), 269–307.

[41] Biographical data on Alabama supreme court judges are available in Lucien D. Gardner, "Chief Justice Edward Spann Dargan," *Alabama Historical Quarterly,* II

What was true in Alabama and Georgia was generally true in the other states of the area. Even in the democratic era of electing judges by popular vote, men of property and community standing continued to sit on the high courts.[42] Although district judges were not as wealthy or as well known on a state basis as the supreme court justices, they, too, were men of some standing and position. A survey of district judges in Texas, for instance, shows the names of some of the state's most able leaders in the antebellum period: William B. Ochiltree, R. E. B. Baylor, John Hancock, John H. Reagan, and Robert J. Townes, to mention a few.[43]

Although the turnover in personnel on the higher courts was not so high as that in the legislature and in the lower courts, it was a factor even here. In Alabama only three of the thirteen individuals who were elected to the supreme court in the 1850's completed a full six-year term, the majority serving only two or three years and then resigning for personal reasons. The turnover in Alabama was exceptional, but even in the other states most judges served only a few years. In Louisiana, for instance, Thomas Slidell, chief justice of the supreme court, was the only one of seventeen high court judges to serve more than six years. This tendency prevailed in other states as well. Notable exceptions were William L. Sharkey, who pre-

(Summer, 1940), 124–26; Garrett, *Reminiscences of Public Men in Alabama,* 114–18, 194–95, 264–65, 347–48, 381–82, 385–86, 425–26, 454–55, 524–25, 549, 591–92; Owen, *History of Alabama and Dictionary of Alabama Biography,* II, 454; and manuscript returns of Seventh and Eighth United States Censuses, 1850 and 1860.

[42] In some states the same men who held an appointive position were later chosen by popular election. When judgeships became elective in Texas, for example, the three appointed judges, John Hemphill, Royal T. Wheeler, and Abner S. Lipscomb, were chosen by the voters to continue in their positions on the bench.

[43] Manuscript "Register State, County Officers, 1846 to 1854," in Texas State Archives, Austin.

sided over the Mississippi supreme court for eighteen years, and John Hemphill, who served as chief justice of Texas during the period of the Republic and during the first twelve years of statehood.

☆☆☆☆

# THE COUNTIES

*Nineteenth-Century Democracy in Action*

IN THE EYES of most nineteenth-century southerners, county government was local government. Charles Sydnor in his study of the development of southern sectionalism points out that the majority of southern people in the antebellum period "looked to their counties or, in Louisiana and the low country of South Carolina, to their parishes as the proper units of local government."[1] City government had a limited role and scope —in major cities such as Charleston and New Orleans—but the lower South was primarily rural.

The county is "an ancient institution, a direct descendant of the Anglo-Saxon shire,"[2] and has some counterparts on the European continent, for some sort of substructure is essential in any centralized form of government. The early English colonists in Virginia brought many of their ideas of local government with them to America, and throughout the Colonial period counties were created to serve the needs of settlers at a distance from the various Colonial capitals. By the close of the Colonial era the idea of county government was so firmly

[1] Sydnor, *Development of Southern Sectionalism,* 33. Sydnor notes that counties existed even in Louisiana in the early nineteenth century, but by 1820 they were merely electoral districts. Efforts were made to introduce the county system into the Tidewater area of South Carolina, but this was abandoned in the late eighteenth century. See Robert Dabney Calhoun, "The Origin and Early Development of County-Parish Government in Louisiana," *Louisiana Historical Quarterly,* XVIII (January, 1935), 136–37; and Andrews, *Administrative County Government in South Carolina,* 16–18.

[2] Lee S. Greene and Robert S. Avery, *Government in Tennessee* (Knoxville, 1962), 324.

established in most areas of the South that positions of responsibility on the county level were sought and secured by the most important social and economic leaders of the colonies.[3]

More than five hundred counties—or parishes, as in Louisiana and Tidewater South Carolina—existed in the states of the lower South in the pre-Civil War decade. By state they varied in number from 37 in Florida, to 132 in Georgia, and up to 152 in Texas. They ranged in size from the midgets of western Georgia to the massive, and largely uninhabited, giants of southern Florida and West Texas.[4] In population the variations were even more pronounced, from Zavala County in Texas, with its twenty-six people, to the urban areas around Charleston and New Orleans with their thousands.[5]

### *Traditional Offices*

Although the counties of the lower South varied in size and population, there were remarkable similarities in governmental institutions. This is not so surprising, because most of our governmental machinery has been built upon Anglo-Saxon custom and tradition. An Englishman visiting South Carolina and Georgia in the early nineteenth century would have found offices that were readily familiar to him. As they were in England itself, the sheriff, the constable, the coroner, and the justices of the peace were traditional figures in southern county government.

Of all the ancient local offices still extant, few if any are

[3] Francis B. Simkins, *A History of the South* (New York, 1963), 50. See also Herbert S. Duncombe, *County Government in America* (Washington, 1966), 18–20.

[4] Although one Louisiana parish, Calcasieu, was as large as any county in Florida.

[5] Based upon Eighth Census of United States, vol. I, *Population.*

older than the office of sheriff. Although his powers were perhaps not as great as in the upper South, the antebellum sheriff in the lower South was still one of the most important local officials. In most states he was charged with enforcing the laws, ordinances, and regulations of the state and county, executing warrants, managing the county jail, and supervising elections.[6] In the states of the upper South he was usually also the tax collector and treasurer of the county. At one time he was charged with these responsibilities in the lower South, but in the nineteenth century most states in the region created separate offices of tax collector and treasurer.[7]

The sheriff worked closely with the administrative body of the county, usually known in the upper South as the county court but commonly called by some other name in the lower South. In Georgia, this unit was known as the inferior court; in Alabama, the commissioners' court of revenue and roads; in Florida, the board of commissioners; in Louisiana, the police jury; and in South Carolina, the commissioners of roads and bridges. In Mississippi this body was originally called the county court, but in 1832 it was renamed the board of police. Only in the frontier state of Texas, where the Virginia and

[6] The sheriff's powers and duties are found in Cobb, *Digest of Statute Laws of Georgia,* 543–77; Thompson, *A Manual or Digest of the Statute Law of Florida,* 60–62; John A. Aiken, *A Digest of Laws of the State of Alabama . . .* (Philadelphia, 1833), 387–88; *Revised Code of the Statute Laws of the State of Mississippi,* 71, 91–92, 120–28; Phillips, *Revised Statutes of Louisiana,* 523–26; Gammel, *The Laws of Texas,* II, 1571–1675.

[7] See Andrews, *Administrative County Government in South Carolina,* 18; and V. O. Key, "A History of Texas County Government" (M.A. thesis, University of Texas, 1930), 48. Compare the southern sheriff's duties with those of his English predecessor in Wallace Notestein, *The English People on the Eve of Colonization, 1603–1630* (New York, 1954), 202–210.

Tennessee influence was strong, was the county administrative unit still known as the county court in the pre-Civil War decade.

The idea of separation of powers, which is so embedded in our mythology concerning governmental structure that it seems to many a self-evident truth, had little validity in southern (or northern) county government. The county unit, whether called county court, board of commissioners, or police jury, exercised legislative, executive, and administrative and judicial functions. Although there were some slight variations, this body performed the same services in most states: supervising elections, establishing ferries, laying out roads, building bridges, appointing and maintaining slave patrols, caring for the poor, maintaining public buildings, licensing liquor retailers, levying the county tax, regulating taverns and houses of entertainment, and establishing quarantine and health regulations.[8] At one time the county courts exercised considerable judicial power, but by the 1850's most of these functions had been transferred to other officers, except in the case of Georgia. In some states the board also had educational duties. In Louisiana, for example, the police jury was charged with leasing school lands;[9] in Texas the county court constituted a board of

[8] For the duties of the county unit see Robert and George Watkins, *A Digest of the Laws of the State of Georgia . . .* (Philadelphia, 1800), 254; Cobb, *Digest of Statute Laws of Georgia,* 952; Hughes, *County Government in Georgia,* 13–17; Grice, "The Old Inferior Court," 5–14; C. C. Clay, *A Digest of the Laws of the State of Alabama . . .* (Tuskaloosa [*sic*], 1843), 506–14; Alexander B. Meek, *A Supplement to Aiken's Digest of the State of Alabama* (Tuscaloosa, 1841), 310–22; Thompson, *Manual or Digest of the Statute Law of Florida,* 126–27; *Revised Code of the Statute Laws of the State of Mississippi,* 171–73, 193–98, 414–20.

[9] Phillips, *Revised Statutes of Louisiana,* 408–11.

school commissioners empowered to create school districts within the county.[10]

The meetings of the county units were of considerable interest to the people because practically all county business was conducted there. As a result the monthly, or in some cases quarterly, sessions of the board were the center of local interest and brought rural southerners into the county seat for business and entertainment. The actual business of the board varied from county to county and meeting to meeting. The minutes of some sessions of police juries in Louisiana, for example, indicate little business transacted, while the minutes of others indicate a full agenda.[11] The minutes of Pointe Coupee police jury for October 27, 1856, show that on that date jurors

[10] Many of the published inventories of county records for Texas have good descriptions of the county court and its functions. See especially Texas Historical Records Survey, *Inventory of the County Archives,* No. 94, *Guadalupe County* (San Antonio, 1939), 105–13, and No. 202, *Sabine County* (San Antonio, 1939), 50–58. See also Gammel, *Laws of Texas,* II, 1639–44, and III, 113–26; Dick Smith, "The Development of Local Government Units in Texas" (Ph.D. dissertation, Harvard University, 1938), 30–31; and Wallace C. Murphy, *County Government and Administration in Texas* (*University of Texas Bulletin,* No. 3324; Austin, 1933), 9–12.

[11] For the 1850–60 period the jury minutes of Iberville and Jefferson have been published. Historical Records Survey, *Transcriptions of Parish Records of Louisiana,* No. 24, *Iberville Parish,* Ser. 1, Police Jury Minutes, vol. I, 1850–62 (Baton Rouge, 1940); and No. 26, *Jefferson Parish,* Ser. I, Police Jury Minutes, vol. III, 1858–70 (New Orleans, 1939). However, in the Department of Archives, Louisiana State University, handwritten and typed copies of jury minutes which cover at least part of the period are available. By parish these are Ascension (1837–56), Avoyelles (1843–52), Assumption (1848–53), Bienville (1856–69), Bossier (1859–66), Caddo (1844–47), Caldwell (1852–55), Calcasieu (1847–67), Catahoula (1857–85), Claiborne (1849–84), DeSoto (1853–70), East Baton Rouge (1847–68), Franklin (1843–55), Lafayette (1823–57), Lafourche (1841–62), Ouachita (1857–67), Pointe Coupee (1848–57), Sabine (1843–65), St. Charles (1854–61), St. Helena (1856–63), St. James (1849–55), St. John the Baptist (1849–82), St. Martin (1843–55), Tensas (1843–58), Terrebone (1854–68), Union (1852–69), West Baton Rouge (1858–80), and West Feliciana (1840–55).

adopted regulations pertaining to the parish attorney, parish auditor, police of slaves, marks and brands of livestock, taverns and grogshops, bakers and butchers, election precincts, parish printer, clerk of the jury, guardian of the courthouse, jailer, physician of the jail, constable, parish tax collector, ferries, fences, and hunting and fishing.[12] Practically every session of the juries devoted some time to the regulation of slaves and free Negroes, particularly in reference to the parish police patrol. And the building of new courthouses and jails resulted in even longer sessions as the endless details of financing, constructing, and furnishing were considered. Through their minutes the reader can follow the progress of these parish projects; for example, the minutes of the St. Charles police jury for May 6, 1854, show that a parish referendum had indicated the voters' approval of the construction of a new parish courthouse. On that date the jury took steps to hire an architect, and a new parish tax was levied to defray the cost of construction. Each monthly session of the jury thereafter devoted some time to the courthouse project. Seven months later the minutes show the work was completed as the jury ordered the sheriff to take possession of the new building. At the same time the jury authorized its president to purchase office signs, draperies, lightning rods, and three dozen spitting boxes for the new building.[13]

In neighboring Mississippi the board of police labored with similar problems. The December, 1859, session of the Adams County board, for example, confined itself to hearing petitions from numerous free Negroes regarding pending action of the state legislature, selecting the January grand jury, and receiv-

[12] Police Jury Minutes, Pointe Coupee Parish, vol. 1848–57, p. 281.

[13] Police Jury Minutes, St. Charles Parish, vol. V, 1848–57, pp. 28–30, 52–58.

ing various accounts for road building and printing.[14] In March of the following year, however, the board meeting was longer because the group not only received various accounts for road building and bridge repairing but also appointed new grand jurors, a county solicitor, and election officials; considered at some length the matter of confinement of lunatics within the county; and authorized payments for hauling freight and corn to the county poorhouse, for making an index to the county deeds, and for county salaries for the past year.[15]

A frequent problem mentioned in Louisiana police jury minutes was that of obtaining a quorum of members present so that parish business could be conducted. The minutes of Tensas Parish show that on June 3, 1850, the jury was forced to adjourn for lack of a quorum. After a threat that absent members would be fined, a quorum was found, and on the next day the business of the parish proceeded. But the problem was not completely solved, for running throughout the minutes of the parish in the 1850's are repeated references to the subject. In St. Charles Parish the problem was so pressing that the names of absent members were turned over to the parish attorney for legal action, and the absentees were fined thirty dollars.

The bulk of county or parish expenditures was directed toward payment of building bonds, salaries and per diem for parish officers, election fees, and relief of the poor. Most of the southern courts conducted all county business on an annual budget of from $2,000 to $5,000. In 1854 the budget of Sabine

[14] Natchez *Daily Courier,* December 13, 1859.

[15] *Ibid.,* March 6, 1860. For representative sessions of the police board see the October 12, 1859, and November 2, 1859, issues of the *Courier.* See also the Vicksburg *Weekly Whig,* October 20, 1858, November 23, 1859, April 4, 1860, June 6, 1860, and July 25, 1860, for sessions of the police board in Warren County.

Parish in Louisiana, for example, was $3,000, while that in Ascension Parish was $3,887.40. Franklin Parish, on the other hand, managed to operate on $1,261 in 1850.[16] However, by 1853, operating expenses in this parish were more than $2,000.[17]

South Carolina differed from the other states of the area in that no one group of officials was responsible for the services mentioned above. Here several commissions, members of which were chosen by and answerable to the legislature, performed the majority of local functions. Among the special commissions were those of public schools, courthouses and jails, naval stores, tobacco inspection, and roads and bridges. The commissioners of roads and bridges were the most important local administrators in South Carolina, because they not only maintained roads, bridges, and ferries, but they also levied taxes and licensed tavern-keepers, retail liquor dealers, and billiard table operators.[18] The legislation dealing with roads and bridges alone was so massive that an attempt was made in 1825 to bring a measure of unity to the functioning of these commissions throughout the state. But by mid-century there was again just as much confusion.[19]

These commissioners of roads were chosen by the legislature after receiving recommendations from the Committee on Vacant Offices. So numerous were the commissioners that only by formal petition of friends or by the individual seeking appoint-

16 Police Jury Minutes, Sabine Parish, vol. I, 1843–65, p. 281; Police Jury Minutes, Ascension Parish, vol. I, 1837–56, p. 343.

17 Police Jury Minutes, Franklin Parish, vol. I, 1843–55, pp. 178, 262.

18 Sydnor, *Growth of Southern Sectionalism,* 43; William A. Schaper, "Sectionalism and Representation," 383.

19 *Statutes at Large of South Carolina,* IX, 558–60.

ment could one's name be brought before the legislature for consideration. The legislative journals for the late antebellum period are filled with such petitions and appointments. Comparison of these names with names of legislators for the period shows that many of the road commissioners either had been or would serve in the assembly. Too, there were many commissioners who bore the same family names as members of the legislature.[20]

Located at the county seat and working under the county court were various lesser officials who operated the machinery of government. Among these were the coroner, who held inquests in cases of violent or sudden death; the surveyor, who surveyed roads and boundaries for the county; the tax collector, who had by the 1850's taken over duties originally performed by the sheriff; and the county clerk, who was the recorder for the county court and kept the county's records. In addition, each county had numerous justices of the peace, who exercised minor judicial power, and constables, who helped in keeping the peace, aided in enforcing the law, and executed civil and criminal processes as directed by the justices of the peace.[21]

20 This does not appear to have been as commonplace, however, as that found by Sydnor, *Growth of Southern Sectionalism,* 47–48, in his study of states in the upper South. For names of commissioners see, for example, *Reports and Resolutions of the General Assembly . . . at the Annual Session of 1851* (Columbus, 1851), 232–44, and *Reports and Resolutions of the General Assembly . . . at the Annual Session of 1856* (Columbia, 1856), 272–85.

21 *Revised Code of the Statute Laws of Mississippi,* 134–36; Aiken, *Digest of Laws of State of Alabama,* 299–301; A. W. Bell, *The State Register: Comprising an Historical and Statistical Account of Louisiana . . .* (Baton Rouge, 1855), 70; Phillips, *Revised Statutes of Louisiana,* 105–106; Gammel, *Laws of Texas,* II, 1567–70.

## *Centralization and Decentralization*

At the beginning of the nineteenth century most local officials in the lower South were named by central authorities. As noted earlier, the legislature in South Carolina selected all local officers, including the various commissioners charged with county administration. In neighboring Georgia the members of the inferior court were chosen by the legislature until 1812 when a constitutional amendment gave this power to the people.[22] The inferior court in turn appointed tax receivers, tax collectors, justices of the peace, treasurers, notaries public, and constables for the county.[23] In Mississippi the Constitution of 1817 provided for the popular election of the sheriff and coroner in each county; but other local officers, including members of the county court, constables, justices of the peace, surveyors, and collectors, were chosen by the legislature.[24] In Louisiana justices of the peace, sheriffs, and most other local officers were appointed by the governor; but some members of the parish police jury were popularly elected.[25]

Only in Alabama were the majority of local officials popularly elected before the 1830's. Here, the liberal Constitution of 1819 provided that the commissioners of revenue and roads, sheriffs, county clerks, justices of the peace, and constables be chosen by the people rather than the central authorities.[26] But

[22] Thorpe, *Federal and State Constitutions,* II, 804; Saye, *Constitutional History of Georgia,* 165–66.

[23] Justices of the peace were also made elective in 1812. Watkins, *Digest of Laws of the State of Georgia,* 467; Cobb, *Digest of Statute Laws of Georgia,* 200–204; and Hughes, *County Government in Georgia,* 13–17.

[24] Thorpe, *Federal and State Constitutions,* IV, 2040–42.

[25] *Ibid.,* III, 1385; and Sydnor, *Development of Southern Sectionalism,* 39.

[26] Most of these officers held office for a three-year term. See Aiken, *Digest of Laws of State of Alabama,* 82, 86–87, 100, 245, 299, 387; and McMillan, *Constitutional Development in Alabama,* 66–67.

even in Alabama, a state at the forefront of the democratic movement, the county judge was elected by the legislature until 1850.

## *Effects of Jacksonian Democracy*

Constitutional revisions in the 1830's and 1840's, resulting from the democratic movements sweeping the country, caused significant changes in southern county government. The shift to widespread popular election with a broadening of the right to vote meant greater responsiveness to the electorate generally. Decentralization was promoted by the process of democratization.

Mississippi with its new Constitution of 1832 eliminated all property, tax, and militia requirements for voting on the state and county levels and replaced the appointed county court with a five-man board of police whose members were popularly elected for the term of two years. In addition, the new constitution provided for the popular election of constables, justices of the peace, surveyors, and collectors—all formerly appointed by the legislature.[27]

The Louisiana constitutions of 1845 and 1852, while not as liberal as those in Alabama and Mississippi, provided for popular election of most local officers. The police jury had already become an entirely elective body by a statute excluding the appointed parish judge. By the new constitutions, justices of the peace, sheriffs, coroners, and constables also became elective positions.[28]

As new states came into existence in the late antebellum

[27] Thorpe, *Federal and State Constitutions,* IV, 2056–57; Drake, "Constitutional Development in Mississippi," 153.

[28] Phillips, *Revised Statutes of Louisiana,* 105–110, 299–307, 523–26.

period, the effects of this "new" democracy were evident in county government. In Texas members of the county court, sheriffs, treasurers, coroners, surveyors, clerks, and tax assessor-collectors were all popularly elected for the term of two years.[29] In Florida, which began statehood with a progressive constitution, the board of commissioners, justices of the peace, sheriffs, clerks, coroners, and constables were all chosen by the people for a two-year term.[30]

Thus, by the 1850's most local officers in the lower South were directly elected by the people. South Carolina, the most highly centralized state in the region, still resisted many of the changes, though, as the legislature still retained the real power in county affairs by means of a series of special commissions. Too, coroners and justices of the peace in South Carolina continued to be selected by the legislature. But even in conservative South Carolina there were some modifications, and by the 1850's the people in each parish or district elected their sheriffs, probate judges, court clerks, tax collectors, and commissioners for the poor.[31]

The Jacksonian concept of rotation in office was widely accepted in the counties of the lower South. The membership of the county administrative units, for example, was constantly changing. In Florida only 110 of the 642 men who served as county commissioners in the 1850–60 period held office for more than one term. And only 40 of these served for more than two terms. Of these, 30 served three terms, 7 served four

[29] Gammel, *Laws of Texas,* II, 1567–75, 1604–14, 1644–46.

[30] Although the probate judge appointed by the governor was an ex-officio member and president of the board of commissioners. Thompson, *A Manual or Digest of the Statute Law of Florida,* 60–62, 126–27.

[31] *Statutes at Large of South Carolina,* V, 569, VI, 12; Andrews, *Administrative County Government in South Carolina,* 17–18.

terms, and 3 men served five terms.[32] The turnover was equally high in Texas. In the period 1854–61, 1,397 individuals served as county commissioners, and of this number only 231, or 16.5 per cent, held office more than one term. One hundred and eighty-nine Texas commissioners served two terms during the period, 37 served three terms, and 4 served four terms.[33]

Rotation in office was also common in the older states of the area. A survey of the rosters of Louisiana police juries, Mississippi boards of police, Alabama justices of the peace, and Georgia inferior court justices, sheriffs, and justices of the peace indicates a rapid turnover of officers in those states.[34] In some cases, especially in the term of office for sheriffs, this turnover was due in part to constitutional or statute prohibitions to re-election.[35] Whatever the reason, be it constitutional restriction, the belief in the democratic concept of rotating governmental personnel, or simply a desire to escape the time-

32 Based on examination of the typewritten copy of the "Roster of State and County Officers of Florida," Florida State Library, Tallahassee.

33 Based on the manuscript "Election Register, 1854–1861," in the Texas State Archives, Austin.

34 Based on police jury minutes for twenty parishes in the Department of Archives, Louisiana State University; "Register of Commissions, State of Mississippi, 1853–1857, 1858–1864," in the Mississippi Department of Archives and History, Jackson; "Civil Register of County Officials, 1844–1867," vol. III, in Alabama Department of Archives and History, Montgomery; "Georgia Executive Department, Commission Book, Justices of the Peace, 1853–1861," and "Georgia Executive Department, Commission Book, County Officers, 1850–1861," in Georgia Department of Archives and History, Atlanta.

35 In most of the states of the lower South the sheriff was prohibited from seeking immediate re-election. In Alabama there were efforts in the legislature to eliminate this constitutional restriction, but the proposed amendment failed to gain two-third's approval necessary before submission to the people. McMillan, *Constitutional Development in Alabama,* 67–68. In Texas the sheriff could be re-elected but could not serve more than four years out of six. Thorpe, *Federal and State Constitutions,* VI, 3555. Even here, however, only 74 of 314 sheriffs elected in the period 1854–61 served a second term.

consuming and little rewarding burden of public service, this turnover in personnel meant that large numbers of southerners were serving in county government in the late antebellum period.

The turnover in county personnel did mean that new faces were serving in various positions of responsibility. In Georgia, for example, only 168 of the 660 inferior court judges serving in 1860, or 25.5 per cent, had had previous experience. Of these, 109 had served only one previous term, 43 had served two terms, 9 had served three terms, 3 had served four terms, 2 had served five terms, and 2, Joseph Donaldson of Cherokee and Waters Briscoe of Walton, had served six previous terms. It should be noted, however, that in most Georgia counties at least one of the five members of the inferior court had previously served, thus providing a small measure of continuity for each term of the court.[36]

Even with the democratic reforms of the Jacksonian period there continued to be strong ties between the state and county governments. In most cases, especially in South Carolina, the elected county officials still looked to the state legislature for advice and direction, just as the earlier appointed county officials had.[37] In Georgia the constitution clearly permitted inferior court justices to serve in the legislature.[38] This practice of serving both as legislator and justice was rather common in the early nineteenth century but was less frequent by the pre-

[36] The names of justices of the inferior court may be found in "Georgia Executive Department, Commission Book, Justices of the Inferior Court, 1813–1861," Georgia Department of Archives and History, Atlanta.

[37] Again this does not appear to be as commonplace as found by Sydnor, *Growth of Southern Sectionalism,* 47–48, in his study of the upper South.

[38] See Sec. 11, Article I of the Constitution of 1798. Thorpe, *Federal and State Constitutions,* II, 792.

Civil War decade. Even so, four senators and fourteen representatives in Georgia also served as inferior court justices in 1850, and eight senators and twelve representatives served in a dual capacity as legislator and judge in 1860. Criticism of this practice continued throughout the nineteenth century, but no amendment prohibiting it was ever adopted.[39]

## *Social and Economic Characteristics of County Officials*

The majority of individuals serving in county government in the pre-Civil War decade were middle-aged. For example, the median age for more than 150 South Carolina road commissioners taken from fourteen sample districts in the 1850's was forty-three years.[40] This is identical with the median age for more than 900 Georgia inferior court judges and more than 200 Mississippi police board members for the same period. Police jurors in Louisiana (median age forty-one years), county court members in Texas (median age forty years), county commissioners in Florida (median age forty-one years), and county sheriffs in Alabama (median forty-one years) were only slightly younger.[41]

As was true in the case of state legislators, the great majority of county officials in the pre-Civil War decade were born in the

[39] Saye, *Constitutional History of Georgia,* 167–68.

[40] The author attempted to make a representative sampling of both low country parishes and up country districts. The low country parishes used were Prince William's (Beaufort), Christ Church and St. James' Santee (Charleston), St. Bartholomew's (Colleton), Prince George's, Winyah (Georgetown), Orange (Orangeburgh), and Clarendon (Sumter). Up country districts used were Anderson, Abbeville, Chesterfield, Fairfield, Lancaster, Marion, and Richland. Personal data on these and other local officials are based largely upon manuscript returns of Seventh and Eighth United States Censuses, 1850 and 1860.

[41] C. J. W. Thorpe, inferior court judge in McIntosh County, Georgia, aged 79 years, was the oldest county official found in this survey of more than three thousand county officers.

South. In the older states, South Carolina and Georgia, the majority of county officials studied were natives of their state. Thus, in South Carolina 146 of 157 road commissioners, or 92.3 per cent, were native South Carolinians. In Georgia nearly two of every three inferior court judges for 1850 and 1860, 64.6 per cent, were native-born Georgians. Too, the percentage of native-born Georgians serving on the court was increasing during the decade, 59.9 per cent of the members of the 1850 courts born in Georgia as compared to 68.1 per cent for 1860. An additional 289 judges, or 31.1 per cent, were born in other southern states. Thus 891 of 930 Georgia judges whose place of birth could be ascertained, or 95.7 per cent, were born in the slaveholding states.[42]

In the Gulf states the percentage of county officials born in the state was not as high, but even so, the majority of local officials were born in the South. Of those studied, more than 80 per cent of the county commissioners in Florida and more than 70 per cent of the police jurors in Louisiana were natives of the lower South. Nearly two thirds, 65.5 per cent, of the members of the Mississippi police boards were born in the lower South. Twenty of some thirty-six Alabama sheriffs were born in the lower South, and none of them were born outside the slaveholding states.[43] In young Texas, as might be expected, the heavy migration from Tennessee, Kentucky, and Missouri was reflected in the finding that approximately half of more than four hundred members of the county court whose places

[42] In Georgia 53 of 77 sheriffs in 1850 and 76 of 114 sheriffs in 1860 were born in that state. Based on information from manuscript returns of Seventh and Eighth United States Censuses, 1850 and 1860.

[43] The writer was unable to locate complete rosters of Alabama commissioners of revenue and roads. They are not found in the "Civil Register of County Officials, 1844–1867," vol. III, in the Alabama Department of Archives and History.

of birth could be ascertained were born in the upper South.[44] Twenty-two of forty Texas sheriffs serving in 1860 were born in the upper South and eleven others in the lower South.

The majority of county officials were engaged in agriculture as an occupation. Nearly 90 per cent of the South Carolina commissioners studied were farmers or planters, a ratio almost identical with Mississippi where 214 of 240 police board members were engaged in agriculture. In four other states, Georgia, Florida, Louisiana, and Texas, three of every four members of the county administrative boards were farmers or planters.[45]

Surprisingly perhaps, next to agriculture there were more merchants than any other occupational group serving in county administrative positions in the lower South. In Georgia some eighty merchants, or approximately 10 per cent of the total number of justices, served on inferior courts in 1850 and 1860; and in Florida twelve merchants, again approximately 10 per cent, served as county commissioners. In several states physicians were third as an occupational group among administrative officials.

Lawyers, on the other hand, never held local administrative posts in appreciable numbers in any of the states of the lower South. Although 16 of some 92 Texas chief justices (presiding officers of the county court) were lawyers, only 2 of 322 commissioners were. In Georgia 18 attorneys sat on the inferior court, but this represents a mere 2 per cent of those serving

[44] Of 452 members of the Texas county courts studied, 85 were Tennesseans.

[45] The percentages of farmers and planters in each were 75.2 per cent in Georgia, 73.7 per cent in Florida, 77.8 per cent in Louisiana, and 72.2 per cent in Texas. A large number of southern sheriffs listed their occupation in the census returns as planter or farmer; in Georgia, for example, 73 of 110 sheriffs whose enumerations could be located in the census. Twenty-nine were listed simply as sheriff, three as merchant, two as livery stable operators, one as a butcher, one as an editor, and one as a grocery keeper.

in 1850 and 1860. None of 122 commissioners in Florida was a lawyer, and only 1 of 240 police board members in Mississippi was a member of this profession.

A large variety of other occupations was listed by county officers. Ministers served on county boards in Georgia, Florida, and Mississippi; mechanics in South Carolina, Georgia, and Louisiana; carpenters in Louisiana and Texas; brickmasons in Mississippi and South Carolina; and laborers in Florida and Louisiana. Seven blacksmiths were members of Georgia inferior courts as were a slave trader, a factor, and a crayonmaker. Five teachers sat on Louisiana police juries in 1860 as did also two engineers and an overseer. Some board members listed other public offices as their occupations. In Texas, for example, at least seven county commissioners were supplementing their incomes by serving as justices of the peace at the same time they held positions on the county court.[46]

Even with the elimination of property requirements for voting and officeholding, the majority of county officials continued to come from the propertied class. This was especially true among members of the county boards. In South Carolina 144 of 157 road commissioners (91.7 per cent) were holders of real property in 1860; and an even greater number in that same year, 155 (98.7 per cent), were holders of personal property.[47] In neighboring Georgia 349 of 384 inferior court members in 1850, or 90.9 per cent, possessed real property;[48] and ten years later the numbers in this same category had risen to 519

[46] These were in Brazos, Burleson, Collin, Hamilton, Hidalgo, Grayson, and Guadalupe counties. "Election Register, 1854–1861."

[47] These figures are based upon examination of the manuscript returns of the Eighth United States Census, 1860.

[48] The reader is reminded that the Seventh United States Census, 1850, did not list individual personal property holdings.

of 547, or 94.9 per cent. In 1860 a total of 530 Georgia inferior judges, or 96.9 per cent, held personal property in addition to real property. In Mississippi the percentages of property holders among police board members were equally high, 94.4 per cent holding real property and 97.4 per cent holding personal property.

TABLE 8

REAL PROPERTY HOLDING OF MEMBERS OF SOUTHERN COUNTY GOVERNING BODIES, 1860

| *Real Property Held* | *No Property* | *Less than $5,000* | *$5,000 to $24,999* | *$25,000 to $99,999* | *$100,000 and more* | *Total* |
|---|---|---|---|---|---|---|
| South Carolina Comm. | 13 | 51 | 68 | 20 | 5 | 157 |
| Georgia Inferior Court * | 59 | 503 | 335 | 32 | 2 | 931 |
| Florida County Comm. | 19 | 70 | 31 | 5 | 0 | 125 |
| Mississippi Police Board | 15 | 121 | 75 | 21 | 3 | 235 |
| Louisiana Police Jury * | 33 | 108 | 53 | 25 | 11 | 230 |
| Texas County Court | 63 | 289 | 90 | 13 | 0 | 455 |

* Includes both 1850 and 1860 members

In three states, Louisiana, Florida, and Texas, the percentage of real property holders among members of parish or county boards was noticeably lower—85.6 per cent in Louisiana, 84.8 per cent in Florida, and 86.2 per cent in Texas. However, the number of personal property owners among these local administrators yielded percentages comparable to the rest of the lower South—97.2 in Louisiana, 96.0 in Florida, and 96.9 in Texas.

The actual amount of property held by most county officials in the pre-Civil War decade was modest, generally less than that held by state legislators. The median real property holding of members of most county administrative boards was $4,000 or less. Only in South Carolina, where the median holding for road commissioners was $7,200, was the figure higher. In three states, Georgia, Mississippi, and Louisiana, the median was exactly $4,000. The median holding in real property among county court members was lowest in the two newest states of the region, Texas ($2,000) and Florida ($1,800).

The majority of county board members held more personal than real property. In two states, Mississippi and Louisiana, the $12,000 median in personal property was three times higher than the median in real property. In three other states, Florida, Georgia, and South Carolina, the median in personal property was at least twice as high as in real property; and in Texas, the personal property holding was nearly twice as high.

Members of the county courts were usually wealthier than other county officials, although undoubtedly there were some exceptions. In Georgia, for example, the typical inferior justice, with $12,000 total property in 1860, held considerably more property than the typical sheriff, with a total median property of $3,300. The same was true in Mississippi, where the median holding for police court members was $16,000, compared to $9,500 for sheriffs.[49] Even so, most county officers of the period did own some form of property. Thus, 315 of 394 sheriffs serving in 1850 and 1860 in the seven states of the lower South,

[49] Based upon data for 114 Georgia and 49 Mississippi sheriffs.

or 79.8 per cent of those studied, held real property, and 300 of 309 sheriffs serving in 1860, or 97.1 per cent, held personal property.[50]

TABLE 9

PERSONAL PROPERTY HOLDING OF MEMBERS OF SOUTHERN COUNTY GOVERNING BODIES, 1860

| *Personal Property Held* | *No Property* | *Less than $5,000* | *$5,000 to $24,999* | *$25,000 to $99,999* | *$100,000 and more* | *Total* |
|---|---|---|---|---|---|---|
| South Carolina Comm. | 2 | 33 | 58 | 54 | 10 | 157 |
| Georgia Inferior Court | 17 | 200 | 230 | 93 | 7 | 547 |
| Florida County Comm. | 5 | 64 | 44 | 10 | 2 | 125 |
| Mississippi Police Board | 6 | 90 | 82 | 51 | 6 | 235 |
| Louisiana Police Jury | 9 | 19 | 33 | 21 | 1 | 83 |
| Texas County Court | 14 | 252 | 166 | 23 | 0 | 455 |

As might be expected, county officials tended to reflect in wealth the counties they served. The wealthier officials came from the rich, heavily slave-populated counties of the black belt, river delta, or coastal areas. In Texas, for example, the

[50] These figures include only sheriffs whose enumerations were located in Schedule No. 1 of the manuscript census returns. Although the author did not make a systematic survey of other county officers, a cursory examination of data for coroners, justices of peace, clerks, and surveyors indicates that the majority of all such officers were small property holders.

only four county commissioners to hold over $100,000 in property in 1860 came from Brazoria and Matagorda counties in the heart of the rich sugar-cotton complex on the lower Brazos and Colorado rivers.[51] Likewise, the wealthiest police jurors in Louisiana came from St. Charles and West Baton Rouge parishes, both prosperous sugar parishes.[52] E. C. Eggleston, wealthiest sheriff in the lower South, lived in Lowndes, Mississippi, a county with more than 70 per cent slave population. In Florida the two wealthiest county commissioners, Joseph Cairnes and George W. Parkhill, came from Leon, the most heavily slave-populated and biggest cotton-producing county in the state.[53] County officers in the less wealthy, sparsely slave-populated counties, on the other hand, usually held less property. The four commissioners from Holmes, a West Florida county with less than 10 per cent slave population, for example, collectively held only $480 in real and $7,186 in personal property in 1860.

More than half the total members of county boards in the lower South during the late antebellum period were slaveholders.[54] The percentage was highest in South Carolina; there, 101

[51] These individuals were R. M. Collins, Joseph Bates, and John Adriance of Brazoria, and George J. Bowie of Matagorda. The greatest concentration of individual wealth in antebellum Texas was in Brazoria, Colorado, Fort Bend, Matagorda, and Wharton counties. See Ralph A. Wooster, "Wealthy Texans, 1860," *Southwestern Historical Quarterly,* LXXI (October, 1967), 163–80.

[52] These were Samuel McCutcheon of St. Charles, who held $350,000 in property, Emile Trinidad of West Baton Rouge, who held $240,000 in property, and Stephen Pipes of West Baton Rouge, who held $247,000 in property.

[53] There were exceptions, of course. Commissioner James Willis of Leon, for example, held only $500 in total property.

[54] Based upon data for 2,459 members of county courts, police juries, etc., from six states (data on Alabama commissioners not available). Of these 2,459 individuals, 1,303, or 52.9 per cent, were slaveholders. Slaveholding based upon manuscript returns of Schedule No. 2, Slave Inhabitants, Eighth United States Census, 1860.

out of 157 road commissioners serving in 1860, or 64.3 per cent, were slaveholders. In four other states, Louisiana, Florida, Georgia, and Mississippi, the percentage of slaveholders was

TABLE 10

SLAVEHOLDERS IN SOUTHERN COUNTY GOVERNING BODIES, 1860

| *Slaves Held* | *None* | *1–9* | *10–19* | *20–49* | *50–99* | *100 and more* | *Total* |
|---|---|---|---|---|---|---|---|
| South Carolina Comm. | 56 | 21 | 18 | 26 | 24 | 12 | 157 |
| Georgia Inferior Court * | 496 | 223 | 172 | 187 | 44 | 8 | 1,130 |
| Florida County Comm. | 55 | 31 | 16 | 19 | 6 | 1 | 128 |
| Mississippi Police Board | 135 | 49 | 42 | 36 | 18 | 2 | 282 |
| Louisiana Police Jury * | 100 | 57 | 33 | 35 | 10 | 5 | 240 |
| Texas County Court | 315 | 131 | 46 | 23 | 7 | 0 | 522 |

*Includes both 1850 and 1860 members

also high: 140 of 240 Louisiana police jurors serving in 1850 and 1860, or 58.8 per cent; 74 of 128 Florida commissioners serving in 1860, or 57.8 per cent; 634 of 1,130 Georgia inferior court judges serving in 1850 and 1860, or 56.1 per cent; and 147 of 282 Mississippi police court members serving in 1860, or 52.1 per cent. Only in Texas, where 207 of 522 county court members (39.5 per cent) were slaveholders, did slaveholders constitute less than half of the members of the county court.

In two states studied where 1850 and 1860 percentages may

be compared, the ratio of slaveholders to non-slaveholders was increasing in the prewar decade. In one of the two states, Georgia, the percentages were nearly the same, 55.5 per cent slaveholders in 1850 and 56.7 per cent slaveholders in 1860. In the other state, Louisiana, however, the increase in the percentage of slaveholders was more substantial, from 49.3 per cent of the 1850 police jurors to 71.5 per cent in 1860.

Although most of the county board members were small slaveholders, nearly one out of five owned twenty or more slaves and thus properly could be classified as planters.[55] More planters served in county government in South Carolina than elsewhere; 62 of the 157 road commissioners, or 39.6 per cent, held twenty or more slaves. The smallest percentage of planters, as was true of slaveholders in general, was in Texas, where only 30 of some 522 members of the county court, or 5.8 per cent, owned twenty or more slaves.[56]

The planters serving on court boards tended to come from counties with a heavy concentration of slaves in the total population. In Florida, for example, all but six of the twenty-six commissioners who owned twenty or more slaves lived in one of the six counties in which slaves constituted more than half of the total population. Only two of the six other planter-commissioners lived in counties in which less than a third of the total population were slaves.[57] And in Mississippi, forty-nine

[55] Four hundred fifty-five of the 2,459 county court members studied held twenty or more slaves.

[56] There were 231 planters, or 21.2 per cent, among members of the Georgia inferior court; 140 planters, or 20.6 per cent, among Louisiana police jurors; 26 planters, or 20.3 per cent, among Florida commissioners; and 56 planters or 19.5 per cent, among members of the Mississippi police boards.

[57] Population figures based upon Eighth Census of United States, vol. I, *Population,* 50–53.

of the fifty-nine planter-police board members lived in counties with 50 per cent or more slaves.

Of some 439 southern sheriffs, 181, or 41.2 per cent, were also slaveholders in the late antebellum period. Again the percentage was highest in South Carolina, where two of every three 1860 sheriffs were slaveholders, and lowest in Texas, where only one of every four sheriffs was a slaveholder. Nineteen of the sheriffs, or 4.3 per cent, held twenty or more slaves in 1860.

## *County Government on the Eve of War*

The personnel and structure of county governments in the lower South on the eve of the Civil War were much alike. Although there was still some measure of state control and direction, particularly in South Carolina, the bulk of county affairs was conducted by local boards chosen directly by the white electorate. These boards, consisting of both slaveholders and non-slaveholders, planters and plain folk, were basically susceptible to the wishes of the citizenry. There were instances where one family played a predominant role in county affairs, sometimes through political influence and other times through domination of the county governmental machinery; but these cases were the exception to the general rule. The fact that there were no property qualifications for voting and that all county offices, except those in South Carolina, were elective meant that the majority of southern whites had an opportunity to participate directly in county affairs. The rapid turnover in personnel, plus the fact that in many states there were more officers, especially justices of the peace, than actually required for county business, meant that literally thousands of persons participated in some form of local government in this decade. For good or bad this constant shifting of personnel meant that new people were directing the governmental machinery, sitting on the county courts, serving the legal papers, keeping the peace, and auditing the books. Here was nineteenth-century political democracy in action.

☆☆☆☆☆

# CLOSE OF AN ERA

*The Lower South on the Eve of War*

THE SECESSION of the states of the lower South from the Union in 1860–61 and the ensuing years of civil war and reconstruction brought to an end an era of substantial political reform on the state and county level. In at least five of the seven states (Mississippi, Texas, Alabama, Florida, and Georgia), privileges of voting and officeholding had been extended, and one could say that democratic government, at least in the nineteenth-century sense, existed. To be sure, Negroes and women did not share these political privileges, and rather formidable residency requirements delayed foreigners and newcomers from full participation in the governmental process. But for most adult white males the structure of government in the five states was democratic.

Mississippi and Texas had gone further than others in political reform by abolishing all property qualifications for voting and officeholding, by making executive, legislative, and judicial offices elective, and by providing for reasonably fair apportionment based upon the white population. Alabama, an early leader in the reform movement, had fallen slightly behind Mississippi and Texas in the 1850's through her failure to provide for popular election of supreme court judges and some state administrative officers. But otherwise Alabama was in the vanguard of progressive reform: there were no property qualifications for voting or officeholding, most state and county officers were elected by the people, and a regular apportionment was based on white population.

Florida was only slightly behind Alabama in the degree of popular participation in state and county government, and in one respect, popular election of all judges, she was ahead of her northern neighbor. But as in Alabama, some state administrative officers were still chosen by the legislature rather than by the people. More important, apportionment in Florida, unlike that in Alabama, was based on the Federal Ratio, which gave a disproportionate voice in state affairs to the big slave counties in the middle part of the state. In this respect Florida resembled her other northern neighbor, Georgia, which also used the Federal Ratio. Georgia, like Alabama, had in the 1820's been one of the most democratic states in the South, but had fallen behind in the march of reform. Although property qualifications had long since been dropped, her constitution in 1860 still required that voters pay "all taxes which may be required of them," and judges and some administrative officers were still chosen by the legislature rather than by the people.

Progress in democratic reform had been made in the 1830's and 1840's, but Louisiana at the beginning of the Civil War still lagged behind five of the cotton states. In some respects she appeared more democratic than others: no property qualifications for voting and officeholding existed, and the principal state and parish officers were elected by the people. The new Constitution of 1852, however, was a regressive step, as its makers fully intended. Under it, apportionment in both houses of the legislature was based on total population, a feature which gave control of the state to a coalition of New Orleans merchants and black belt planters and offset many of the democratic gains of an earlier period.

South Carolina, one of the two oldest states in the region, had made some progress by extending the suffrage to all white males who met a residency requirement and by making some minor offices, such as sheriff, elective. But on the whole it resisted the changes of the early nineteenth century. There were still substantial property requirements for holding state office, the legislature rather than the people continued to choose the governor and presidential electors of the state, and county government remained thoroughly undemocratic. On the eve of the Civil War, South Carolina was still the "stronghold of the landed aristocracy" and the least democratic state in the lower South.

In all of the states of the lower South, whether conservative or democratic, the center of governmental activity was the state legislature. As we have noted, variations did exist as to the extent of legislative authority. In South Carolina, for example, the legislature exercised vast appointive power and virtually controlled local as well as state government, whereas in Mississippi and Texas its powers were confined more to the lawmaking area. But even in these more democratic states the legislature was clearly the dominant branch of government.

Requirements for serving in the legislature had been gradually reduced in the first half of the nineteenth century. Property barriers were dropped in all states of the lower South with the exception of South Carolina, which still required resident senators and representatives to possess a freehold estate of 300 and 150 pounds sterling, respectively, and nonresident senators and representatives to possess 1,000 and 500 pounds sterling, respectively. All of the states had some type of state residency requirement, usually two or three years, as well as a local residency requirement of usually one year.[1] Two states, Florida

[1] Thorpe, *A Constitutional History of the American People,* I, 425, points out that the residency requirement was usually longer in the slave states than in the northern

and Alabama, had the same residency requirements for senators as for representatives; the other four had longer residency requirements for senators than for representatives. All of the states, with the exception of South Carolina which called for state citizenship only, required that legislators be citizens of the United States. Several states either still had or previously had had constitutional provisions excluding duelists from legislative service. Mississippi's constitution barred all who did not believe in God from holding any public office; Texas' constitution excluded ministers of the gospel from legislative service (but not, it appears, from holding other offices); and Florida's constitution prohibited duelists, ministers, and bank presidents from serving as governor or legislator.

The individuals who served in the antebellum legislatures were generally middle-aged farmers, planters, and lawyers. State senators were usually two or three years older on the average than were state representatives, and legislators serving in 1860 were on the average a year or two older than those serving in 1850. The South Carolina senates of both 1850 and 1860 and the Mississippi senate of 1860 had the highest median ages; the Texas house of 1850 had the lowest median age. The differences in age between various legislatures were so slight, however, that little significance should be attached to this factor.

The great majority of legislators were born in the slaveholding states and usually in the lower South. In only two of the seven states of the region, Louisiana and Texas, were more than 10 per cent of the legislators born outside the South. Too, the percentage of non-southerners serving in the legislature

states. Volume II, 409–12, of this work has charts showing qualifications for legislators by state, 1800 to 1850.

was lower in 1860 than in 1850 in all of the states of the area with the exception of Texas. The percentages of legislators born in the upper South also dropped in the pre-Civil War decade.[2]

The number of slaveholders serving in all the legislatures did increase in the pre-Civil War decade. As we have seen, this increase was particularly significant in the rich, expanding states of the Southwest—Alabama, Mississippi, Louisiana, and Texas. By 1860 slaveholders constituted a majority in every legislature of the lower South.

The number of planters (those with twenty or more slaves) in the state legislatures also increased in the 1850 decade, except in Georgia. The increase was slight in South Carolina and Louisiana, but was more than 10 per cent in Alabama, Mississippi, and Texas. Even so, planters held numerical superiority only in the South Carolina legislature. In Mississippi the division between planters and non-planters in the legislature was almost even by 1860. In only one other state, Alabama, did planters occupy more than one third of the seats in the pre-Civil War legislature.

The fact that most southern legislators served only one term in office meant that the majority of them had little role in setting policy or guiding through major legislation. Real power rested in the hands of those members who through years of service became chairmen of the more important committees. In some states, Texas for example, individual leaders active primarily on the national scene, such as Sam Houston and Thomas J. Rusk, held together loose coalitions which functioned sufficiently well on specific issues to pass legislation

[2] With the single exception of South Carolina, where there was an increase of 0.3 per cent in the decade.

at the state level.[3] In others, such as Louisiana where political boss John Slidell ruled, power rested with party leaders who exercised control in both state and national affairs. However, except in South Carolina, where the plantation elite continued to rule, and to some extent in Louisiana, the masses of southern whites had sufficient strength as a result of the wave of democratic reforms to make passage of legislation hostile to their interests, real or supposed, very difficult.[4]

The disintegration of the Whig party in the 1850's gave Democrats control of all the state legislatures in the lower South. This does not mean, of course, that there was no opposition. In all of the states except South Carolina some form of opposition group continued to support legislative candidates throughout the 1850 decade. The American, or Know Nothing, party made a particularly strong bid in Georgia, Alabama, Louisiana, and Texas in the mid-fifties; and a so-called "Opposition" faction, consisting of former Whigs, Know Nothings, and Independents, continued to oppose the Democrats in most legislatures as late as 1860. Many Whigs, of course, went over to the Democratic party prior to secession. Socio-economic differences between Whigs and Democrats in the late antebellum period were never so great in the lower South as to form a real barrier to those who wished to cross party lines.

Although a few Whigs and a considerable number of Know Nothings continued to gain election to the state legislatures, the Democrats had a monopoly on the governorship in all states of the lower South in the 1850's. Of some thirty gover-

[3] The Thomas J. Rusk Papers, University of Texas Archives, Austin, for example, are filled with correspondence pertaining to political matters on the state level.

[4] See, for example, Clanton W. Williams, "Early Ante-Bellum Montgomery: A Black Belt Constituency," *Journal of Southern History,* VII (August, 1941), 522.

nors who were elected in the period 1849 to 1861 only one, Thomas G. Brown of Florida, was a Whig; all others were Democrats.[5]

As in the case of legislators, the various states differed slightly in the constitutional requirements for the governorship. South Carolina was the only one still retaining a property qualification, but Georgia dropped a similar qualification as late as in 1847. In all but South Carolina the governor was elected by the people, and in all but Louisiana, where the minimum age was lowered to twenty-eight years in 1852, a minimum age of thirty years was required. There were varying residency and citizenship requirements. South Carolina stipulated only that the governor be a citizen and resident of the state for ten years, but the other states called for United States citizenship for a period of several years prior to election. Mississippi required the governor to have been a citizen for twenty years, and Alabama required that he be a *native* citizen of the United States. In three states, South Carolina, Florida, and Louisiana, the chief executive served a four-year term but was ineligible for immediate re-election. In three others, Alabama, Mississippi, and Texas, he held office for two years and was eligible for immediate re-election, but could serve only four years of every six. In only one state, Georgia, where the governor served a two-year term, were there no limitations as to re-election.

Gubernatorial power in every state of the lower South was severely limited. Although the governor could recommend legislation, was commander of the state's militia, and had some

[5] Senator John Guion, who, as president of the Mississippi senate, served out the remaining part of John A. Quitman's term, was also a Whig; but he was not an elected governor.

pardoning and appointive powers, he was definitely secondary to the legislature. In no state could he appoint judges or principal administrative officers after 1852; and in only four states, Georgia, Mississippi, Louisiana, and Texas, did he have a real veto power. In South Carolina there was no veto at all, and in Florida and Alabama the governor's veto could be overridden by a simple majority of the legislature.

The structure of the judiciary in the pre-Civil War lower South was significantly similar in the seven states. By 1860 some type of supreme tribunal existed in all the states—each had circuit or district courts, and all had probate and justice of the peace courts. In three states, South Carolina, Florida, and Alabama, equity cases were still heard in special courts, and in a fourth state, Mississippi, separate courts existed for equity cases up until 1856.

Different methods for choosing judges still prevailed in the prewar decade. In Mississippi, Florida, and Texas (after 1850) all judges were chosen by the people for six-year terms.[6] In Louisiana judges were also chosen by the voters after 1852, but for eight years in the case of the supreme court and four years for district courts. In Alabama supreme court judges were chosen by the legislature for six-year terms, but a constitutional amendment in 1850 provided for the popular election of circuit court judges. In Georgia the legislature still chose all the judges for the high state courts, with supreme court judges serving six-year terms and superior court judges serving three-year terms. In conservative South Carolina, which had one of the most complex higher court systems, judges were chosen by the legislature for a period of good behavior.

[6] Except circuit court judges in Mississippi who served four-year terms.

County government in the 1850 decade was democratic in all of the lower South with the exception of South Carolina. In the Palmetto state sheriffs, probate judges, tax collectors, and commissioners for the poor had come to be popularly elected by 1850, but the real power in local affairs remained in the hands of the state legislature. Through a system of special commissions, especially the commission of roads and bridges, in each district or parish the legislature continued to control most local activity. The commissioners themselves were elected by the legislature, were in many cases bound to the legislature by personal or family ties, and were at all times accountable to the legislature.

County government in the other states of the region was similar. In each there were several popularly elected local officials including justices of the peace, probate judges, sheriffs, constables, coroners, tax collectors, county clerks, and surveyors; but the real power in county affairs rested in an administrative body known in Georgia as the inferior court, in Florida as the board of commissioners, in Alabama as the commissioners' court of revenue and roads, in Mississippi as the board of police, in Louisiana as the police jury, and in Texas as the county court. These bodies consisted of five members per county in each state except Louisiana, where size varied from parish to parish, and by 1850 the members of all were elected popularly for two-year terms. Powers and duties of the county administrative bodies were similar from state to state: building roads, policing of slaves, regulating taverns and inns, passing livestock ordinances, levying county fines and taxes, establishing bridges and ferries, and in general conducting county affairs.

Throughout the lower South the individuals who served on these county governing bodies resembled somewhat the state legislators, except in one or two respects. Legislators had slightly larger holdings of personal and real property than did county officials, and in all states except Louisiana the legislators had larger holdings of slaves. Except in Texas, a majority of the members of county administrative boards in the lower South were slaveholders, but only in Louisiana was the percentage of slaveholders on the local board higher than that in the state's legislature. As might be expected, it was generally true that more county board members than legislators were born in the lower South and more were engaged in agriculture. As in the case of legislators there was a heavy turnover in membership on the county boards from year to year.

Overall, the structure of state and county government in the lower South on the eve of the Civil War was, in the nineteenth-century sense, democratic. In five of the seven states most of the major state officers were elected by the people, and property and tax qualifications had been abolished. In a sixth state, Louisiana, there was much that was democratic, but legislative apportionment was not truly representative of the people. In South Carolina an aristocracy still controlled state and county affairs.

Thousands of southerners actively participated in their government in the pre-Civil War decade, partly because of the plethora of local offices, especially justices of the peace, but mainly because of a widespread tendency to serve only one term in office. Indeed, rotation in office may have been the most striking characteristic of southern government for the period. Certainly the tendency for eight of ten legislators and three of four county officials to serve only one term is in marked contrast to the present South where long tenure in office appears to be commonplace.[7]

Certain general similarities did exist among southern officeholders on the eve of secession—mostly they were middle-aged, born in the South, holders of real and personal property. The diversities, though, are much more striking and make generalization regarding the social characteristics of those who held public office difficult. Three points do appear clear: first, legislators and other public officials in the lower South were predominantly agrarian in their sympathies and outlook; second, both planters and plain people played an active role in state and county government in the late antebellum period; and third, a larger number of slaveholders and planters held public office in 1860 than in 1850.[8] Whether tendencies and trends evident in the 1850's would have continued no one can say. Lincoln's election and the secession of the states of the lower South from the Union closed an era in southern history and directed attention away from legislative halls toward the fields of battle.

[7] Although William E. Oden, "Tenure and Turnover in Recent Texas Legislatures," *Southwestern Social Science Quarterly,* XLV (March, 1965), 371–74, points out that 39.5 per cent of the members of the Texas legislature for the period 1935–61 had no previous experience in the legislature.

[8] It should be noted that with the exception of Florida and Georgia there was a slightly higher percentage of slaveholders and planters in the total population of states in the lower South in 1860 than in 1850. However, the percentages of increase for both slaveholders and planters serving in state and county government were considerably higher than the percentage of increase in the total population.

# APPENDIX I

*Personal Characteristics of Southern Legislators*

TABLE II

AGE OF MEMBERS OF ALABAMA LEGISLATURE

*1850*

| *Age* * | *House* | *Senate* | *Totals* |
|---|---|---|---|
| 20–29 years | 13 | 4 | 17 |
| 30–39 | 36 | 5 | 41 |
| 40–49 | 29 | 16 | 45 |
| 50–59 | 15 | 4 | 19 |
| 60–69 | 1 | 2 | 3 |
| Totals | 94 | 31 | 125 |

*1860*

| *Age* * | *House* | *Senate* | *Totals* |
|---|---|---|---|
| 20–29 years | 10 | 2 | 12 |
| 30–39 | 29 | 14 | 43 |
| 40–49 | 29 | 13 | 42 |
| 50–59 | 15 | 5 | 20 |
| 60–69 | 3 | 3 | 6 |
| 70–79 | | 1 | 1 |
| Totals | 86 | 38 | 124 |

* Age ascertained for 125 of 134 legislators in 1850 and 124 of 135 legislators in 1860.

TABLE 12

PLACE OF BIRTH OF MEMBERS OF ALABAMA LEGISLATURE

| Place of Birth * | House | Senate | Totals |
|---|---|---|---|
| *1850* | | | |
| South Carolina | 24 | 9 | 33 |
| Georgia | 21 | 6 | 27 |
| Alabama | 13 | 4 | 17 |
| Virginia | 11 | 2 | 13 |
| Tennessee | 7 | 5 | 12 |
| North Carolina | 10 | 1 | 11 |
| Others [1] | 8 | 3 | 11 |
| Totals | 94 | 30 | 124 |
| *1860* | | | |
| Georgia | 30 | 7 | 37 |
| Alabama | 21 | 8 | 29 |
| South Carolina | 16 | 6 | 22 |
| North Carolina | 7 | 2 | 9 |
| Virginia | 7 | 2 | 9 |
| Tennessee | 4 | 4 | 8 |
| Others [2] | 3 | 2 | 5 |
| Totals | 88 | 31 | 119 |

* Place of birth ascertained for 124 of 134 legislators in 1850 and 119 of 135 legislators in 1860.

[1] Includes two born in New York, two born in Vermont, two born in England, and one each born in Kentucky, Maryland, Connecticut, Massachusetts, and Scotland.

[2] Includes three born in Kentucky, and one each born in Ohio and New Hampshire.

TABLE 13

OCCUPATION OF MEMBERS OF ALABAMA LEGISLATURE

| *Occupation* * | *House* | *Senate* | *Totals* |
|---|---|---|---|
| *1850* | | | |
| Planter or Farmer | 57 | 13 | 70 |
| Lawyer | 23 | 8 | 31 |
| Minister | 3 | 2 | 5 |
| Physician | 3 | 1 | 4 |
| Merchant | 3 | 1 | 4 |
| Others [1] | 3 | 2 | 5 |
| Totals | 92 | 27 | 119 |
| *1860* | | | |
| Planter or Farmer | 47 | 19 | 66 |
| Lawyer | 19 | 7 | 26 |
| Physician | 6 | | 6 |
| Merchant-Planter | 2 | 2 | 4 |
| Others [2] | 11 | 2 | 13 |
| Totals | 85 | 30 | 115 |

* Occupation ascertained for 119 of 134 legislators in 1850 and 115 of 135 legislators in 1860.

[1] Includes one printer, one wheelwright, one miller, one teacher, and one lumberman.

[2] Includes three merchants, three lawyer-planters, three manufacturers, one editor, one carpenter, one railroad president, and one lawyer-editor.

TABLE 14

REAL PROPERTY HOLDING OF MEMBERS OF ALABAMA LEGISLATURE

*1850*

| *Real Property* * | *House* | *Senate* | *Totals* |
|---|---|---|---|
| No property listed | 16 | 5 | 21 |
| Less than $5,000 | 44 | 12 | 56 |
| $5,000 and less than $25,000 | 24 | 10 | 34 |
| $25,000 and less than $100,000 | 9 | 1 | 10 |
| $100,000 and more | | 1 | 1 |
| Totals | 93 | 29 | 122 |

*1860*

| *Real Property* * | *House* | *Senate* | *Totals* |
|---|---|---|---|
| No property listed | 8 | 1 | 9 |
| Less than $5,000 | 33 | 8 | 41 |
| $5,000 and less than $25,000 | 32 | 8 | 40 |
| $25,000 and less than $100,000 | 14 | 10 | 24 |
| $100,000 and more | 1 | 3 | 4 |
| Totals | 88 | 30 | 118 |

* Property holding ascertained for 122 of 134 legislators in 1850 and 118 of 135 legislators in 1860.

TABLE 15

PERSONAL PROPERTY HOLDING OF MEMBERS OF ALABAMA LEGISLATURE

*1860*

| *Personal Property* * | *House* | *Senate* | *Totals* |
|---|---|---|---|
| No property listed | 8 | 1 | 9 |
| Less than $5,000 | 16 | 5 | 21 |
| $5,000 and less than $25,000 | 23 | 6 | 29 |
| $25,000 and less than $100,000 | 33 | 9 | 42 |
| $100,000 and more | 8 | 9 | 17 |
| Totals | 88 | 30 | 118 |

* Property holding ascertained for 118 of 135 legislators.

TABLE 16

SLAVE HOLDINGS OF MEMBERS OF ALABAMA LEGISLATURE

*1850*

| *Slaves* | *House* | *Senate* | *Totals* |
|---|---|---|---|
| None | 34 | 11 | 45 |
| 1–9 | 20 | 5 | 25 |
| 10–19 | 15 | 9 | 24 |
| 20–49 | 16 | 5 | 21 |
| 50–99 | 9 | 3 | 12 |
| 100 and more | 6 | 1 | 7 |
| Totals | 100 | 34 | 134 |

*1860*

| *Slaves* | *House* | *Senate* | *Totals* |
|---|---|---|---|
| None | 26 | 6 | 32 |
| 1–9 | 24 | 7 | 31 |
| 10–19 | 13 | 4 | 17 |
| 20–49 | 19 | 5 | 24 |
| 50–99 | 14 | 7 | 21 |
| 100 and more | 6 | 4 | 10 |
| Totals | 102 | 33 | 135 |

TABLE 17

SLAVE HOLDINGS OF POLITICAL FACTIONS IN ALABAMA LEGISLATURE

*1850*

| *Slaves* | *Whigs* | *Democrats* | *Totals* |
|---|---|---|---|
| None | 19 | 26 | 45 |
| 1–9 | 8 | 17 | 25 |
| 10–19 | 12 | 12 | 24 |
| 20–49 | 9 | 12 | 21 |
| 50–99 | 6 | 6 | 12 |
| 100 and more | 4 | 3 | 7 |
| Totals | 58 | 76 | 134 |

TABLE 18

AGE OF MEMBERS OF FLORIDA LEGISLATURE

*1860*

| *Age* * | *House* | *Senate* | *Totals* |
|---|---|---|---|
| 20–29 years | 5 | 1 | 6 |
| 30–39 | 15 | 6 | 21 |
| 40–49 | 14 | 3 | 17 |
| 50–59 | 5 | 1 | 6 |
| 60–69 | | 1 | 1 |
| Totals | 39 | 12 | 51 |

* Age ascertained for 39 of 46 house members and 12 of 20 senate members.

TABLE 19

PLACE OF BIRTH OF MEMBERS OF FLORIDA LEGISLATURE

*1860*

| *Place of Birth* * | *House* | *Senate* | *Totals* |
|---|---|---|---|
| South Carolina | 10 | 4 | 14 |
| Georgia | 11 | 2 | 13 |
| Florida | 8 | 2 | 10 |
| North Carolina | 6 | | 6 |
| Others [1] | 2 | 3 | 5 |
| Totals | 37 | 11 | 48 |

* Place of birth ascertained for 37 of 46 house members and 11 of 20 senate members.

[1] Includes one each born in Tennessee, Kentucky, New York, New Jersey, and Ireland.

TABLE 20

OCCUPATION OF MEMBERS OF FLORIDA LEGISLATURE

*1860*

| *Occupation* * | *House* | *Senate* | *Totals* |
|---|---|---|---|
| Farmer or Planter | 25 | 9 | 34 |
| Lawyer | 4 | 2 | 6 |
| Physician | 4 | | 4 |
| Merchant | 3 | 1 | 4 |
| Surveyor | 1 | | 1 |
| Livery Stable | | 1 | 1 |
| Totals | 37 | 13 | 50 |

* Occupation ascertained for 37 of 46 house members and 13 of 20 senate members.

TABLE 21

PROPERTY HOLDING OF MEMBERS OF FLORIDA LEGISLATURE

*1860*

| *Real Property* * | *House* | *Senate* | *Totals* |
|---|---|---|---|
| No property listed | 8 | | 8 |
| Less than $5,000 | 16 | 4 | 20 |
| $5,000 and less than $25,000 | 13 | 6 | 19 |
| $25,000 and less than $100,000 | 2 | 2 | 4 |
| Totals | 39 | 12 | 51 |

| *Personal Property* * | *House* | *Senate* | *Totals* |
|---|---|---|---|
| No property listed | 4 | | 4 |
| Less than $5,000 | 14 | | 14 |
| $5,000 and less than $25,000 | 17 | 6 | 23 |
| $25,000 and less than $100,000 | 3 | 5 | 8 |
| $100,000 and more | 1 | 1 | 2 |
| Totals | 39 | 12 | 51 |

* Property holding ascertained for 39 of 46 house members and 12 of 20 senate members.

TABLE 22

SLAVE HOLDINGS OF MEMBERS OF FLORIDA LEGISLATURE

*1860*

| *Slaves* | *House* | *Senate* | *Totals* |
|---|---|---|---|
| None | 23 | 6 | 29 |
| 1–9 | 11 | 6 | 17 |
| 10–19 | 4 | 2 | 6 |
| 20–49 | 5 | 2 | 7 |
| 50–99 | 1 | 1 | 2 |
| 100 and more | 2 | 2 | 4 |
| Totals * | 46 | 19 | 65 |

* No census returns available for one senator and one representative.

TABLE 23

AGE OF MEMBERS OF GEORGIA LEGISLATURE

*1850*

| *Age* * | *House* | *Senate* | *Totals* |
|---|---|---|---|
| 20–29 years | 13 | 5 | 18 |
| 30–39 | 48 | 13 | 61 |
| 40–49 | 42 | 10 | 52 |
| 50–59 | 14 | 9 | 23 |
| 60–69 | 1 | 2 | 3 |
| Totals | 118 | 39 | 157 |

*1860*

| *Age* * | *House* | *Senate* | *Totals* |
|---|---|---|---|
| 20–29 years | 19 | 10 | 29 |
| 30–39 | 53 | 38 | 91 |
| 40–49 | 60 | 38 | 98 |
| 50–59 | 11 | 22 | 33 |
| 60–69 | 6 | 8 | 14 |
| Totals | 149 | 116 | 265 |

* Age ascertained for 157 of 175 legislators in 1850 and 265 of 293 legislators in 1860.

TABLE 24

PLACE OF BIRTH OF MEMBERS OF GEORGIA LEGISLATURE

| Place of Birth * | House | Senate | Totals |
|---|---|---|---|
| | *1850* | | |
| Georgia | 78 | 27 | 105 |
| South Carolina | 19 | 4 | 23 |
| North Carolina | 17 | 5 | 22 |
| Virginia | 4 | 3 | 7 |
| Totals | 118 | 39 | 157 |
| | *1860* | | |
| Georgia | 112 | 86 | 198 |
| South Carolina | 18 | 13 | 31 |
| North Carolina | 14 | 7 | 21 |
| Virginia | 4 | 4 | 8 |
| Others [1] | 3 | 6 | 9 |
| Totals | 151 | 116 | 267 |

* Place of birth ascertained for 157 of 175 legislators in 1850 and 267 of 293 legislators in 1860.

[1] Includes two born in Tennessee, two born in Kentucky, and one each born in Massachusetts, New York, England, France, and Ireland.

TABLE 25

OCCUPATION OF MEMBERS OF GEORGIA LEGISLATURE

| *Occupation* * | *House* | *Senate* | *Totals* |
|---|---|---|---|
| *1850* | | | |
| Planter or Farmer | 73 | 25 | 98 |
| Lawyer | 20 | 8 | 28 |
| Physician | 7 | 3 | 10 |
| Merchant | 6 | 1 | 7 |
| Others [1] | 8 | 2 | 10 |
| Totals | 114 | 39 | 153 |
| *1860* | | | |
| Planter or Farmer | 102 | 72 | 174 |
| Lawyer | 25 | 23 | 48 |
| Physician | 7 | 6 | 13 |
| Merchant | 1 | 4 | 5 |
| Others [2] | 14 | 10 | 24 |
| Totals | 149 | 115 | 264 |

* Occupation ascertained for 153 of 175 legislators in 1850 and 264 of 293 legislators in 1860.

[1] Includes two lawyer-farmers, two teachers, one mechanic, one wheelwright, one tavernkeeper, one hatter, one hotelkeeper, and one clergyman.

[2] Includes three lawyer-farmers, three lawyer-planters, three ministers, three teachers, two hotelkeepers, two landlords, two carpenters, one physician-planter, one mechanic-planter, one port collector, one justice, one railroad conductor, and one warehouseman.

TABLE 26

REAL PROPERTY HOLDING OF MEMBERS OF GEORGIA LEGISLATURE

*1850*

| *Real Property* * | *House* | *Senate* | *Totals* |
|---|---|---|---|
| No property listed | 12 | 4 | 16 |
| Less than $5,000 | 58 | 17 | 75 |
| $5,000 and less than $25,000 | 45 | 15 | 60 |
| $25,000 and less than $100,000 | 3 | 3 | 6 |
| Totals | 118 | 39 | 157 |

*1860*

| *Real Property* * | *House* | *Senate* | *Totals* |
|---|---|---|---|
| No property listed | 11 | 2 | 13 |
| Less than $5,000 | 79 | 43 | 122 |
| $5,000 and less than $25,000 | 55 | 51 | 106 |
| $25,000 and less than $100,000 | 3 | 19 | 22 |
| $100,000 and more | 1 | | 1 |
| Totals | 149 | 115 | 264 |

* Property holding ascertained for 157 of 175 legislators in 1850 and 264 of 293 legislators in 1860.

TABLE 27

PERSONAL PROPERTY HOLDING OF MEMBERS OF GEORGIA LEGISLATURE

*1850*

| *Personal Property* * | *House* | *Senate* | *Totals* |
|---|---|---|---|
| No property listed | 1 | 2 | 3 |
| Less than $5,000 | 50 | 27 | 77 |
| $5,000 and less than $25,000 | 73 | 47 | 120 |
| $25,000 and less than $100,000 | 22 | 37 | 59 |
| $100,000 and more | 2 | 3 | 5 |
| Totals | 148 | 116 | 264 |

* Property holding ascertained for 264 of 293 legislators in 1860.

TABLE 28

SLAVE HOLDINGS OF MEMBERS OF GEORGIA LEGISLATURE

*1850*

| *Slaves* | *House* | *Senate* | *Totals* |
|---|---|---|---|
| None | 37 | 16 | 53 |
| 1–9 | 31 | 6 | 37 |
| 10–19 | 26 | 7 | 33 |
| 20–49 | 28 | 11 | 39 |
| 50–99 | 3 | 7 | 10 |
| 100 and more | 3 | | 3 |
| Totals | 128 | 47 | 175 |
| *1860* | | | |
| None | 50 | 33 | 83 |
| 1–9 | 38 | 33 | 71 |
| 10–19 | 36 | 18 | 54 |
| 20–49 | 31 | 28 | 59 |
| 50–99 | 10 | 12 | 22 |
| 100 and more | 1 | 3 | 4 |
| Totals | 166 | 127 | 293 |

TABLE 29

SLAVE HOLDINGS OF POLITICAL FACTIONS IN GEORGIA LEGISLATURE

*1850*

| *Slaves* | *Whigs* | *Democrats* | *Totals* |
|---|---|---|---|
| None | 17 | 24 | 41 |
| 1–9 | 11 | 17 | 28 |
| 10–19 | 17 | 10 | 27 |
| 20–49 | 20 | 13 | 33 |
| 50–99 | 8 | 1 | 9 |
| 100 and more | 1 | 2 | 3 |
| Totals | 74 | 67 | 141 |

TABLE 30

AGE OF MEMBERS OF LOUISIANA LEGISLATURE

| *Age* * | *House* | *Senate* | *Totals* |
|---|---|---|---|
| *1850* | | | |
| 20–29 years | 12 | 1 | 13 |
| 30–39 | 28 | 10 | 38 |
| 40–49 | 11 | 6 | 17 |
| 50–59 | 10 | 4 | 14 |
| 60–69 | 3 | 1 | 4 |
| Totals | 64 | 22 | 86 |
| *1860* | | | |
| 20–29 years | 10 | 3 | 13 |
| 30–39 | 20 | 7 | 27 |
| 40–49 | 32 | 9 | 41 |
| 50–59 | 14 | 3 | 17 |
| 60–69 | 4 | — | 4 |
| Totals | 80 | 22 | 102 |

* Age ascertained for 86 of 122 legislators in 1850 and 102 of 127 legislators in 1860.

TABLE 31

PLACE OF BIRTH OF MEMBERS OF LOUISIANA LEGISLATURE

*1850*

| *Place of Birth* * | *House* | *Senate* | *Totals* |
|---|---|---|---|
| Louisiana | 21 | 8 | 29 |
| Kentucky | 6 | 2 | 8 |
| Virginia | 5 | 2 | 7 |
| Tennessee | 5 | 2 | 7 |
| Georgia | 6 | | 6 |
| South Carolina | 4 | 1 | 5 |
| Mississippi | 4 | 1 | 5 |
| Others [1] | 13 | 6 | 19 |
| Totals | 64 | 22 | 86 |

*1860*

| *Place of Birth* * | *House* | *Senate* | *Totals* |
|---|---|---|---|
| Louisiana | 29 | 9 | 38 |
| Mississippi | 10 | 1 | 11 |
| Virginia | 5 | 1 | 6 |
| South Carolina | 4 | 1 | 5 |
| North Carolina | 4 | 1 | 5 |
| New York | 2 | 3 | 5 |
| Tennessee | 4 | | 4 |
| Others [2] | 18 | 6 | 24 |
| Totals | 76 | 22 | 98 |

* Place of birth ascertained for 86 of 122 legislators in 1850 and 98 of 127 legislators in 1860.

[1] Includes two each born in North Carolina, New Jersey, New York, New Hampshire, and Ireland, and one each born in Alabama, Maryland, Arkansas, Delaware, Ohio, Pennsylvania, Vermont, England, and Germany.

[2] Includes three each born in Alabama, Kentucky, and Georgia; two each born in Missouri, Arkansas, and Pennsylvania; and one each born in Maryland, District of Columbia, Indiana, Massachusetts, Canada, England, France, Scotland, and Germany.

TABLE 32

OCCUPATION OF MEMBERS OF LOUISIANA LEGISLATURE

| Occupation * | House | Senate | Totals |
|---|---|---|---|
| *1850* | | | |
| Farmer or Planter | 26 | 10 | 36 |
| Lawyer | 13 | 6 | 19 |
| Merchant | 3 | 1 | 4 |
| Physician | 1 | 2 | 3 |
| Notary Public | 3 | | 3 |
| Others [1] | 14 | 2 | 16 |
| Totals | 60 | 21 | 81 |
| *1860* | | | |
| Farmer or Planter | 42 | 12 | 54 |
| Lawyer | 16 | 3 | 19 |
| Merchant | 4 | | 4 |
| Physician | 2 | 2 | 4 |
| Others [2] | 12 | 3 | 15 |
| Totals | 76 | 20 | 96 |

* Occupation ascertained for 81 of 122 legislators in 1850 and 96 of 127 legislators in 1860.

[1] Includes two lumber mill owners, two editors, two state officials, one brick mason, one cooper, one blacksmith, one mechanic, one shipwright, one ferryman, one recorder, one hunter, one speculator, and one sheriff.

[2] Includes two farmer-physicians, two editors, two gentlemen, one blacksmith, one surveyor, one printer, one clerk, one engineer, one druggist, one builder, one accountant, and one agent.

TABLE 33

REAL PROPERTY HOLDING OF MEMBERS OF LOUISIANA LEGISLATURE

*1850*

| *Real Property* * | *House* | *Senate* | *Totals* |
|---|---|---|---|
| No property listed | 18 | 3 | 21 |
| Less than $5,000 | 19 | 4 | 23 |
| $5,000 and less than $25,000 | 16 | 7 | 23 |
| $25,000 and less than $100,000 | 10 | 5 | 15 |
| $100,000 and more | 2 | 3 | 5 |
| Totals | 65 | 22 | 87 |

*1860*

| *Real Property* * | *House* | *Senate* | *Totals* |
|---|---|---|---|
| No property listed | 10 | 4 | 14 |
| Less than $5,000 | 14 | 4 | 18 |
| $5,000 and less than $25,000 | 26 | 7 | 33 |
| $25,000 and less than $100,000 | 18 | 4 | 22 |
| $100,000 and more | 10 | 3 | 13 |
| Totals | 78 | 22 | 100 |

* Property holding ascertained for 87 of 122 legislators in 1850 and 100 of 127 legislators in 1860.

TABLE 34

PERSONAL PROPERTY HOLDING OF MEMBERS OF LOUISIANA LEGISLATURE

*1860*

| *Personal Property* * | *House* | *Senate* | *Totals* |
|---|---|---|---|
| No property listed | 6 | 1 | 7 |
| Less than $5,000 | 21 | 5 | 26 |
| $5,000 and less than $25,000 | 25 | 5 | 30 |
| $25,000 and less than $100,000 | 23 | 10 | 33 |
| $100,000 and more | 3 | 1 | 4 |
| Totals | 78 | 22 | 100 |

* Property holding ascertained for 100 of 127 legislators in 1860.

TABLE 35

SLAVE HOLDINGS OF MEMBERS OF LOUISIANA LEGISLATURE

*1850*

| *Slaves* | *House* | *Senate* | *Totals* |
|---|---|---|---|
| None | 60 | 10 | 70 |
| 1–9 | 15 | 4 | 19 |
| 10–19 | 7 | 2 | 9 |
| 20–49 | 8 | 4 | 12 |
| 50–99 | 3 | 5 | 8 |
| 100 and more | 1 | 3 | 4 |
| Totals | 94 | 28 | 122 |

*1860*

| *Slaves* | *House* | *Senate* | *Totals* |
|---|---|---|---|
| None | 35 | 12 | 47 |
| 1–9 | 29 | 3 | 32 |
| 10–19 | 14 | 4 | 18 |
| 20–49 | 19 | 4 | 23 |
| 50–99 | 2 | 2 | 4 |
| 100 and more | 2 | 1 | 3 |
| Totals | 101 | 26 | 127 |

TABLE 36

SLAVE HOLDINGS OF FACTIONS IN LOUISIANA HOUSE OF REPRESENTATIVES

*1850*

| *Slaves* | *Whigs* | *Democrats* | *Totals* |
|---|---|---|---|
| None | 33 | 27 | 60 |
| 1–9 | 7 | 8 | 15 |
| 10–19 | 4 | 3 | 7 |
| 20–49 | 4 | 4 | 8 |
| 50–99 | 1 | 2 | 3 |
| 100 and more | 1 | — | 1 |
| Totals | 50 | 44 | 94 |

TABLE 37

AGE OF MEMBERS OF MISSISSIPPI LEGISLATURE

| Age * | House | Senate | Totals |
|---|---|---|---|
| *1850* | | | |
| 20–29 years | 11 | 2 | 13 |
| 30–39 | 41 | 13 | 54 |
| 40–49 | 16 | 12 | 28 |
| 50–59 | 9 | 2 | 11 |
| 60–69 | 1 | 1 | 2 |
| Totals | 78 | 30 | 108 |
| *1860* | | | |
| 20–29 years | 5 | | 5 |
| 30–39 | 28 | 10 | 38 |
| 40–49 | 19 | 10 | 29 |
| 50–59 | 13 | 4 | 17 |
| 60–69 | 3 | 3 | 6 |
| Totals | 68 | 27 | 95 |

* Age ascertained for 108 of 122 legislators in 1850 and 95 of 109 legislators in 1860.

TABLE 38

PLACE OF BIRTH OF MEMBERS OF MISSISSIPPI LEGISLATURE

| Place of Birth * | House | Senate | Totals |
|---|---|---|---|
| *1850* | | | |
| South Carolina | 13 | 9 | 22 |
| Tennessee | 12 | 4 | 16 |
| Mississippi | 10 | 5 | 15 |
| Georgia | 11 | | 11 |
| Virginia | 6 | 5 | 11 |
| North Carolina | 9 | | 9 |
| Alabama | 8 | | 8 |
| Others [1] | 9 | 6 | 15 |
| Totals | 78 | 29 | 107 |
| *1860* | | | |
| Tennessee | 12 | 3 | 15 |
| South Carolina | 11 | 4 | 15 |
| Mississippi | 9 | 5 | 14 |
| Alabama | 10 | 2 | 12 |
| North Carolina | 7 | 1 | 8 |
| Georgia | 4 | 4 | 8 |
| Others [2] | 7 | 5 | 12 |
| Totals | 60 | 24 | 84 |

* Place of birth ascertained for 107 of 122 legislators in 1850 and 84 of 109 legislators in 1860.

[1] Includes five born in Kentucky, two in Maryland, two in Scotland, and one each born in Missouri, Ohio, Massachusetts, Connecticut, Maine, and Ireland.

[2] Includes six born in Virginia, three in Kentucky, two in Maryland, and one in Ohio.

TABLE 39

OCCUPATION OF MEMBERS OF MISSISSIPPI LEGISLATURE

| *Occupation* * | *House* | *Senate* | *Totals* |
|---|---|---|---|
| *1850* | | | |
| Farmer or Planter | 50 | 18 | 68 |
| Lawyer | 18 | 8 | 26 |
| Physician | 3 | 3 | 6 |
| Others [1] | 7 | — | 7 |
| Totals | 78 | 29 | 107 |
| *1860* | | | |
| Farmer or Planter | 45 | 15 | 60 |
| Lawyer | 11 | 7 | 18 |
| Physician | 5 | 1 | 6 |
| Others [2] | 5 | 3 | 8 |
| Totals | 66 | 26 | 92 |

* Occupation ascertained for 107 of 122 legislators in 1850 and 92 of 109 legislators in 1860.

[1] Includes three merchants, one teacher, one stock raiser, one saddler, and one cistern digger.

[2] Includes three local officials, two merchants, one manufacturer, one minister, and one master mechanic.

TABLE 40

REAL PROPERTY HOLDING OF MEMBERS OF MISSISSIPPI LEGISLATURE

| Real Property * | House | Senate | Totals |
|---|---|---|---|
| *1850* | | | |
| No property listed | 13 | 4 | 17 |
| Less than $5,000 | 47 | 15 | 62 |
| $5,000 and less than $25,000 | 16 | 10 | 26 |
| $25,000 and less than $100,000 | 2 | | 2 |
| $100,000 and more | 2 | | 2 |
| Totals | 80 | 29 | 109 |
| *1860* | | | |
| No property listed | 9 | 1 | 10 |
| Less than $5,000 | 17 | 7 | 24 |
| $5,000 and less than $25,000 | 24 | 13 | 37 |
| $25,000 and less than $100,000 | 13 | 6 | 19 |
| $100,000 and more | 2 | 1 | 3 |
| Totals | 65 | 28 | 93 |

* Property holding ascertained for 109 of 122 legislators in 1850 and 93 of 109 legislators in 1860.

TABLE 41

PERSONAL PROPERTY HOLDING OF MEMBERS OF MISSISSIPPI LEGISLATURE

*1860*

| Personal Property * | House | Senate | Totals |
|---|---|---|---|
| No property listed | 4 | 1 | 5 |
| Less than $5,000 | 9 | 3 | 12 |
| $5,000 and less than $25,000 | 26 | 9 | 35 |
| $25,000 and less than $100,000 | 22 | 14 | 36 |
| $100,000 and more | 4 | 1 | 5 |
| Totals | 65 | 28 | 93 |

* Property holding ascertained for 93 of 109 legislators in 1860.

TABLE 42

SLAVE HOLDINGS OF MEMBERS OF MISSISSIPPI LEGISLATURE

*1850*

| *Slaves* | *House* | *Senate* | *Totals* |
|---|---|---|---|
| None | 36 | 11 | 47 |
| 1–9 | 19 | 5 | 24 |
| 10–19 | 13 | 5 | 18 |
| 20–49 | 15 | 8 | 23 |
| 50–99 | 3 | 3 | 6 |
| 100 and more | 4 | — | 4 |
| Totals | 90 | 32 | 122 |

*1860*

| *Slaves* | *House* | *Senate* | *Totals* |
|---|---|---|---|
| None | 22 | 7 | 29 |
| 1–9 | 17 | 3 | 20 |
| 10–19 | 9 | 5 | 14 |
| 20–49 | 19 | 10 | 29 |
| 50–99 | 7 | 4 | 11 |
| 100 and more | 5 | 1 | 6 |
| Totals | 79 | 30 | 109 |

TABLE 43

SLAVE HOLDINGS OF FACTIONS IN MISSISSIPPI LEGISLATURE

*1850*

| *Slaves* | *Whigs* | *Democrats* | *Totals* |
|---|---|---|---|
| None | 14 | 24 | 38 |
| 1–9 | 5 | 15 | 20 |
| 10–19 | 5 | 13 | 18 |
| 20–49 | 5 | 14 | 19 |
| 50–99 | 2 | 3 | 5 |
| 100 and more | 3 | 1 | 4 |
| Totals | 34 | 70 | 104 |

TABLE 44

AGE OF MEMBERS OF SOUTH CAROLINA LEGISLATURE

*1850*

| *Age* * | *House* | *Senate* | *Totals* |
|---|---|---|---|
| 20–29 years | 12 | | 12 |
| 30–39 | 37 | 11 | 48 |
| 40–49 | 27 | 27 | 54 |
| 50–59 | 13 | 9 | 22 |
| 60–69 | 6 | 1 | 7 |
| 70 and over | 2 | | 2 |
| Totals | 97 | 48 | 145 |

*1860*

| *Age* * | *House* | *Senate* | *Totals* |
|---|---|---|---|
| 20–29 years | 22 | | 22 |
| 30–39 | 36 | 14 | 50 |
| 40–49 | 31 | 20 | 51 |
| 50–59 | 19 | 9 | 28 |
| 60–69 | | 3 | 3 |
| 70 and over | 2 | 1 | 3 |
| Totals | 110 | 47 | 157 |

* Age ascertained for 145 of 174 legislators in 1850 and 157 of 175 legislators in 1860.

TABLE 45

PLACE OF BIRTH OF MEMBERS OF SOUTH CAROLINA LEGISLATURE

| Place of Birth * | House | Senate | Totals |
|---|---|---|---|
| *1850* | | | |
| South Carolina | 91 | 44 | 135 |
| North Carolina | 2 | | 2 |
| Virginia | 2 | 1 | 3 |
| Others[1] | 3 | 3 | 6 |
| Totals | 98 | 48 | 146 |
| *1860* | | | |
| South Carolina | 102 | 45 | 147 |
| North Carolina | 5 | 1 | 6 |
| Others[2] | 3 | 2 | 5 |
| Totals | 110 | 48 | 158 |

* Place of birth ascertained for 146 of 174 legislators in 1850 and 158 of 175 legislators in 1860.

[1] Includes one each born in Pennsylvania, Massachusetts, Scotland, France, Germany, and at sea.

[2] Includes one each born in Florida, Georgia, Pennsylvania, Scotland, and Ireland.

TABLE 46

OCCUPATION OF MEMBERS OF SOUTH CAROLINA LEGISLATURE

| *Occupation* * | *House* | *Senate* | *Totals* |
|---|---|---|---|
| *1850* | | | |
| Planter or Farmer | 53 | 29 | 82 |
| Lawyer | 25 | 10 | 35 |
| Physician | 8 | 4 | 12 |
| Merchant | 4 | | 4 |
| Others [1] | 5 | 3 | 8 |
| Totals | 95 | 46 | 141 |
| *1860* | | | |
| Planter or Farmer | 60 | 30 | 90 |
| Lawyer | 24 | 8 | 32 |
| Physician | 10 | 2 | 12 |
| Merchant | 5 | 1 | 6 |
| Others [2] | 8 | 5 | 13 |
| Totals | 107 | 46 | 153 |

* Occupation ascertained for 141 of 174 legislators in 1850 and 153 of 175 legislators in 1860.

[1] Includes two who listed occupation as public official, three who were lawyer-planters, and one physician-planter, one merchant-farmer, and one manufacturer.

[2] Includes two physician-planters, two lawyer-planters, one editor-lawyer, one manufacturer, one editor, one machinist, one railroad superintendent, one factor, one minister, one gentleman, and one druggist.

TABLE 47

REAL PROPERTY HOLDING OF MEMBERS OF SOUTH CAROLINA LEGISLATURE

| *Real Property* * | *House* | *Senate* | *Totals* |
|---|---|---|---|
| *1850* | | | |
| No property listed | 9 | 1 | 10 |
| Less than $5,000 | 20 | 9 | 29 |
| $5,000 and less than $25,000 | 52 | 24 | 76 |
| $25,000 and less than $100,000 | 17 | 7 | 24 |
| $100,000 and more | 2 | 3 | 5 |
| Totals | 100 | 44 | 144 |
| *1860* | | | |
| No property listed | 8 | 1 | 9 |
| Less than $5,000 | 25 | 4 | 29 |
| $5,000 and less than $25,000 | 57 | 16 | 73 |
| $25,000 and less than $100,000 | 16 | 18 | 34 |
| $100,000 and more | 3 | 5 | 8 |
| Totals | 109 | 44 | 153 |

* Property holdings ascertained for 144 of 174 legislators in 1850 and 153 of 175 legislators in 1860.

TABLE 48

PERSONAL PROPERTY HOLDING OF MEMBERS OF SOUTH CAROLINA LEGISLATURE

*1860*

| *Personal Property* * | *House* | *Senate* | *Totals* |
|---|---|---|---|
| No property listed | 10 | 4 | 14 |
| Less than $5,000 | 5 | 1 | 6 |
| $5,000 and less than $25,000 | 40 | 7 | 47 |
| $25,000 and less than $100,000 | 40 | 19 | 59 |
| $100,000 and more | 12 | 14 | 26 |
| Totals | 107 | 45 | 152 |

* Property holding ascertained for 152 of 175 legislators.

TABLE 49

SLAVE HOLDINGS OF MEMBERS OF SOUTH CAROLINA LEGISLATURE

| *Slaves* | *House* | *Senate* | *Totals* |
|---|---|---|---|
| *1850* | | | |
| None | 30 | 4 | 34 |
| 1–9 | 19 | 6 | 25 |
| 10–19 | 21 | 1 | 22 |
| 20–49 | 32 | 18 | 50 |
| 50–99 | 13 | 10 | 23 |
| 100–199 | 7 | 8 | 15 |
| 200 and more | 3 | 2 | 5 |
| Totals | 125 | 49 | 174 |
| *1860* | | | |
| None | 28 | 4 | 32 |
| 1–9 | 23 | 1 | 24 |
| 10–19 | 17 | 5 | 22 |
| 20–49 | 32 | 9 | 41 |
| 50–99 | 21 | 19 | 40 |
| 100–199 | 3 | 7 | 10 |
| 200 and more | 3 | 3 | 6 |
| Totals | 127 | 48 | 175 |

TABLE 50

AGE OF MEMBERS OF TEXAS LEGISLATURE

| Age * | House | Senate | Totals |
|---|---|---|---|
| *1850* | | | |
| 20–29 years | 6 | | 6 |
| 30–39 | 21 | 14 | 35 |
| 40–49 | 11 | 7 | 18 |
| 50–59 | 3 | 2 | 5 |
| 60–69 | | 1 | 1 |
| Totals | 41 | 24 | 65 |
| *1860* | | | |
| 20–29 years | 13 | | 13 |
| 30–39 | 27 | 13 | 40 |
| 40–49 | 21 | 10 | 31 |
| 50–59 | 17 | 4 | 21 |
| 60–69 | 6 | 1 | 7 |
| 70 and over | | 1 | 1 |
| Totals | 84 | 29 | 113 |

* Age ascertained for 65 of 80 legislators in 1850 and 113 of 138 legislators in 1860.

TABLE 51

PLACE OF BIRTH OF MEMBERS OF TEXAS LEGISLATURE

*1850*

| *Place of Birth* * | *House* | *Senate* | *Totals* |
|---|---|---|---|
| Tennessee | 9 | 4 | 13 |
| North Carolina | 6 | 4 | 10 |
| Kentucky | 5 | 3 | 8 |
| Georgia | 5 | 2 | 7 |
| Mississippi | 3 | 3 | 6 |
| South Carolina | 5 | 1 | 6 |
| Virginia | 3 | 3 | 6 |
| Others [1] | 7 | 4 | 11 |
| Totals | 43 | 24 | 67 |

*1860*

| *Place of Birth* * | *House* | *Senate* | *Totals* |
|---|---|---|---|
| Tennessee | 21 | 4 | 25 |
| Georgia | 11 | 4 | 15 |
| Virginia | 9 | 5 | 14 |
| Alabama | 4 | 4 | 8 |
| North Carolina | 6 | 1 | 7 |
| Kentucky | 5 | 1 | 6 |
| Texas | 5 | | 5 |
| Mississippi | 3 | 1 | 4 |
| Others [2] | 18 | 9 | 27 |
| Totals | 82 | 29 | 111 |

* Place of birth ascertained for 67 of 80 legislators in 1850 and 111 of 138 legislators in 1860.

[1] Includes two each born in New Jersey and Missouri and one each born in Ohio, Pennsylvania, New Hampshire, New York, Connecticut, Germany, and England.

[2] Includes three each born in Louisiana, South Carolina, Illinois, and Connecticut; two each born in Maryland, Indiana, Pennsylvania, and Germany; and one each born in Arkansas, New York, Massachusetts, Maine, England, Ireland, and Austria.

TABLE 52

OCCUPATION OF MEMBERS OF TEXAS LEGISLATURE

| *Occupation* * | *House* | *Senate* | *Totals* |
|---|---|---|---|
| *1850* | | | |
| Farmer or Planter | 21 | 11 | 32 |
| Lawyer | 9 | 7 | 16 |
| Physician | 4 | 2 | 6 |
| Merchant | 3 | 3 | 6 |
| Others [1] | 4 | | 4 |
| Totals | 41 | 23 | 64 |
| *1860* | | | |
| Farmer or Planter | 41 | 11 | 52 |
| Lawyer | 22 | 8 | 30 |
| Public Official | 5 | 1 | 6 |
| Physician | 3 | 1 | 4 |
| Merchant | 3 | 1 | 4 |
| Others [2] | 10 | 7 | 17 |
| Totals | 84 | 29 | 113 |

* Occupation ascertained for 64 of 80 legislators in 1850 and 113 of 138 legislators in 1860.

[1] Includes one clerk, one printer, one hotelkeeper, and one postmaster.

[2] Includes three land agents, three lawyer-farmers, three printers, two surveyors, two stock raisers, one trader, one druggist, one sportsman, and one soldier.

TABLE 53

REAL PROPERTY HOLDING OF MEMBERS OF TEXAS LEGISLATURE

*1850*

| *Real Property* * | *House* | *Senate* | *Totals* |
|---|---|---|---|
| No property listed | 6 | 3 | 9 |
| Less than $5,000 | 27 | 9 | 36 |
| $5,000 and less than $25,000 | 8 | 8 | 16 |
| $25,000 and less than $100,000 | 1 | 2 | 3 |
| Totals | 42 | 22 | 64 |

*1860*

| *Real Property* * | *House* | *Senate* | *Totals* |
|---|---|---|---|
| No property listed | 10 | 1 | 11 |
| Less than $5,000 | 25 | 11 | 36 |
| $5,000 and less than $25,000 | 32 | 10 | 42 |
| $25,000 and less than $100,000 | 14 | 4 | 18 |
| $100,000 and more | 3 | 3 | 6 |
| Totals | 84 | 29 | 113 |

* Property holding ascertained for 64 of 80 legislators in 1850 and 113 of 138 legislators in 1860.

TABLE 54

PERSONAL PROPERTY HOLDING OF MEMBERS OF TEXAS LEGISLATURE

*1860*

| *Personal Property* * | *House* | *Senate* | *Totals* |
|---|---|---|---|
| No property listed | 4 | | 4 |
| Less than $5,000 | 24 | 5 | 29 |
| $5,000 and less than $25,000 | 35 | 17 | 52 |
| $25,000 and less than $100,000 | 17 | 6 | 23 |
| $100,000 and more | 2 | | 2 |
| Totals | 82 | 28 | 110 |

* Property holding ascertained for 110 of 138 legislators in 1860.

TABLE 55

SLAVE HOLDINGS OF MEMBERS OF TEXAS LEGISLATURE

| Slaves | House | Senate | Totals |
|---|---|---|---|
| *1850* | | | |
| None | 37 | 12 | 49 |
| 1–9 | 12 | 6 | 18 |
| 10–19 | 3 | 5 | 8 |
| 20–49 | 4 | 1 | 5 |
| Totals | 56 | 24 | 80 |
| *1860* | | | |
| None | 45 | 18 | 63 |
| 1–9 | 24 | 8 | 32 |
| 10–19 | 10 | 8 | 18 |
| 20–49 | 18 | 1 | 19 |
| 50–99 | 3 | 2 | 5 |
| 100 and more | 1 | | 1 |
| Totals | 101 | 37 | 138 |

# APPENDIX II

## *Personal Characteristics of Members of Southern County Governing Boards*

TABLE 56

AGE OF JUSTICES OF GEORGIA INFERIOR COURTS

| *Age* | *1850 Justices* | *1860 Justices* | *Totals* |
|---|---|---|---|
| 20–29 years | 20 | 33 | 53 |
| 30–39 | 118 | 135 | 253 |
| 40–49 | 127 | 185 | 312 |
| 50–59 | 95 | 141 | 236 |
| 60–69 | 22 | 47 | 69 |
| 70 and over | 1 | 9 | 10 |
| Totals | 383 | 550 | 933 |

TABLE 57

PLACE OF BIRTH OF JUSTICES OF GEORGIA INFERIOR COURTS

| *Place of Birth* | *1850 Justices* | *1860 Justices* | *Totals* |
|---|---|---|---|
| Georgia | 230 | 372 | 602 |
| South Carolina | 61 | 65 | 126 |
| North Carolina | 47 | 72 | 119 |
| Virginia | 17 | 12 | 29 |
| Tennessee | 5 | 7 | 12 |
| Other Southern States | 1 | 2 | 3 |
| Northern States | 18 | 12 | 30 |
| Foreign Countries | 5 | 4 | 9 |
| Totals | 384 | 546 | 930 |

TABLE 58

OCCUPATION OF JUSTICES OF GEORGIA INFERIOR COURTS

| *Occupation* | *1850 Justices* | *1860 Justices* | *Totals* |
|---|---|---|---|
| Planter or Farmer | 292 | 404 | 696 |
| Merchant | 39 | 47 | 86 |
| Physician | 14 | 20 | 34 |
| Lawyer | 7 | 11 | 18 |
| Minister | 3 | 4 | 7 |
| Blacksmith | 2 | 5 | 7 |
| Teacher | 3 | 2 | 5 |
| Mechanic | 3 | 2 | 5 |
| Hotelkeeper | 1 | 4 | 5 |
| Other occupations | 15 | 48 | 63 |
| Totals | 379 | 547 | 926 |

TABLE 59

REAL PROPERTY HOLDING OF JUSTICES OF GEORGIA INFERIOR COURTS

| *Real Property* * | *1850 Justices* | *1860 Justices* | *Totals* |
|---|---|---|---|
| Less than $1,000 | 68 | 59 | 127 |
| $1,000 and less than $5,000 | 152 | 224 | 376 |
| $5,000 and less than $25,000 | 121 | 214 | 335 |
| $25,000 and less than $100,000 | 11 | 21 | 32 |
| $100,000 and more | 1 | 1 | 2 |
| Totals | 353 | 519 | 872 |

* Property holding ascertained for 872 of 931 justices.

TABLE 60

PERSONAL PROPERTY HOLDING OF JUSTICES OF GEORGIA INFERIOR COURTS

| *Personal Property* * | *1860 Justices* |
|---|---|
| Less than $1,000 | 61 |
| $1,000 and less than $5,000 | 139 |
| $5,000 and less than $25,000 | 230 |
| $25,000 and less than $100,000 | 93 |
| $100,000 and more | 7 |
| Total | 530 |

* Property holding ascertained for 530 of 547 justices.

TABLE 61

SLAVE HOLDINGS OF JUSTICES OF GEORGIA INFERIOR COURTS

| *Slaves* | *1850 Justices* | *1860 Justices* | *Totals* |
|---|---|---|---|
| None | 209 | 287 | 496 |
| 1–9 | 90 | 133 | 223 |
| 10–19 | 72 | 100 | 172 |
| 20–49 | 78 | 109 | 187 |
| 50–99 | 16 | 28 | 44 |
| 100 and more | 5 | 3 | 8 |
| Totals | 470 | 660 | 1,130 |

TABLE 62

PROPERTY HOLDING OF FLORIDA COUNTY COMMISSIONERS

*1860*

| *Real Property* | *Commissioners* |
|---|---|
| No property listed | 19 |
| Less than $5,000 | 70 |
| $5,000 and less than $25,000 | 31 |
| $25,000 and less than $100,000 | 5 |
| Total | 125 |

| *Personal Property* | *Commissioners* |
|---|---|
| No property listed | 5 |
| Less than $5,000 | 64 |
| $5,000 and less than $25,000 | 44 |
| $25,000 and less than $100,000 | 10 |
| $100,000 and more | 2 |
| Total | 125 |

TABLE 63

SLAVE HOLDINGS OF FLORIDA COUNTY COMMISSIONERS

*1860*

| *Slaves* | *Commissioners* |
|---|---|
| None | 55 |
| 1–9 | 31 |
| 10–19 | 16 |
| 20–49 | 19 |
| 50–99 | 6 |
| 100 and more | 1 |
| Total | 128 |

TABLE 64

REAL PROPERTY HOLDING OF MEMBERS OF LOUISIANA POLICE JURIES

| *Real Property* | *Members* |
|---|---|
| No property listed | 33 |
| Less than $5,000 | 108 |
| $5,000 and less than $25,000 | 53 |
| $25,000 and less than $100,000 | 25 |
| $100,000 and more | 11 |
| Total | 230 |

TABLE 65

SLAVE HOLDINGS OF MEMBERS OF LOUISIANA POLICE JURIES

| *Slaves* | *Members* |
|---|---|
| None | 100 |
| 1–9 | 57 |
| 10–19 | 33 |
| 20–49 | 35 |
| 50–99 | 10 |
| 100 and more | 5 |
| Total | 240 |

TABLE 66

PROPERTY HOLDING OF MEMBERS OF MISSISSIPPI POLICE BOARDS

*1860*

| *Real Property* | *Members* |
|---|---|
| No property listed | 15 |
| Less than $5,000 | 121 |
| $5,000 and less than $25,000 | 75 |
| $25,000 and less than $100,000 | 21 |
| $100,000 and more | 3 |
| Total | 235 |

| *Personal Property* | *Members* |
|---|---|
| No property listed | 6 |
| Less than $5,000 | 90 |
| $5,000 and less than $25,000 | 82 |
| $25,000 and less than $100,000 | 51 |
| $100,000 and more | 6 |
| Total | 235 |

TABLE 67

SLAVE HOLDINGS OF MEMBERS OF MISSISSIPPI POLICE BOARDS

*1860*

| *Slaves* | *Members* |
|---|---|
| None | 135 |
| 1–9 | 49 |
| 10–19 | 42 |
| 20–49 | 36 |
| 50–99 | 18 |
| 100 and more | 2 |
| Total | 282 |

TABLE 68

PROPERTY HOLDING OF MEMBERS OF TEXAS COUNTY COURTS

*1860*

| *Real Property* | *County Commissioners* | *Chief Justices* |
|---|---|---|
| No property listed | 55 | 8 |
| Less than $5,000 | 227 | 62 |
| $5,000 and less than $25,000 | 71 | 19 |
| $25,000 and less than $100,000 | 11 | 2 |
| Totals | 364 | 91 |

| *Personal Property* | *County Commissioners* | *Chief Justices* |
|---|---|---|
| No property listed | 10 | 4 |
| Less than $5,000 | 196 | 56 |
| $5,000 and less than $25,000 | 138 | 28 |
| $25,000 and less than $100,000 | 20 | 3 |
| Totals | 364 | 91 |

TABLE 69

SLAVE HOLDINGS OF MEMBERS OF TEXAS COUNTY COURTS

*1860*

| *Slaves* | *County Commissioners* | *Chief Justices* |
|---|---|---|
| None | 257 | 58 |
| 1–9 | 96 | 35 |
| 10–19 | 43 | 3 |
| 20–49 | 21 | 2 |
| 50–99 | 6 | 1 |
| Totals | 423 | 99 |

# BIBLIOGRAPHICAL ESSAY

THE VARIOUS STATE CONSTITUTIONS form the beginning point for a study of state and local government in the late antebellum period. These constitutions and amendments thereto may be found in Francis N. Thorpe (comp.), *The Federal and State Constitutions, Colonial Charters, and other Organic Laws of the States, Territories, and Colonies Now or Heretofore Forming the United States* (7 vols.; Washington, 1909), but must be supplemented by the statutes adopted by the various state governments. For South Carolina these are found in *Statutes at Large of South Carolina, 1682–1866* (13 vols.; Columbia, 1836–1875). There are a number of digests and codifications for Georgia; the author found most satisfactory Robert and George Watkins (comps.), *A Digest of the Laws of the State of Georgia* (Philadelphia, 1800); Horatio Marbury and William H. Crawford (comps.), *Digest of the State of Georgia from Its Settlement as a British Province* (Savannah, 1802); Arthur Foster (comp.), *A Digest of the Laws of the State of Georgia* (Philadelphia, 1831); Oliver H. Prince (comp.), *A Digest of the Laws of Georgia* (Athens, 1837); and T. R. R. Cobb (comp.), *A Digest of the Statute Laws of Georgia* (Athens, 1851). For Florida see Leslie A. Thompson (comp.), *A Manual or Digest of the Statute Laws of the State of Florida* (Boston, 1847). Three sources contain Alabama statutes for the period: C. C. Clay (comp.), *A Digest of the Laws of the State of Alabama* (Tus[c]aloosa, 1843); John G. Aiken (comp.), *A Digest of Laws of the State of Alabama* (Philadelphia, 1833); and Alexander B. Meek (comp.), *A Supplement to*

*Aiken's Digest of the Laws of the State of Alabama* (Tuscaloosa, 1841). For Mississippi the *Revised Code of the Statute Laws of the State of Mississippi* (Jackson, 1857) is a reasonably complete compilation published late enough in the antebellum period to include all vital legislation. For Louisiana see Henry A. Bullard and Thomas Curry (comps.), *A New Digest of the Statute Laws of the State of Louisiana* (New Orleans, 1842), and U. B. Phillips (comp.), *The Revised Statutes of Louisiana* (New Orleans, 1856). There is *A Digest of the Laws of Texas,* compiled by Oliver C. Hartley (Philadelphia, 1850), but this does not cover legislation of the 1850's, which may be found in H. P. N. Gammel (comp.), *The Laws of Texas, 1822–1897* (10 vols.; Austin, 1898).

The printed journals of the various state legislatures and constitutional conventions add much to an understanding of the above mentioned laws and constitutions. Extremely important, too, are the reports, resolutions, and documents printed by legislative bodies. For some states, especially South Carolina, these contain valuable reports of legislative committees which add much information to the study of state and local administration.

## *Sources of Names*

Names of governors, legislators, and supreme court judges may be obtained from legislative journals and state histories, but determining the names of lesser state officers and county officials is a more difficult task. The manuscript "Executive and Legislative Appointment Book," in the South Carolina Archives Department, Columbia, South Carolina, lists some county officers such as sheriff, probate judge, and court clerk; but the *Reports and Resolutions of the General Assembly of*

*South Carolina* for the period must be consulted for names of the important commissioners of roads and bridges. The manuscript "Commissions, County Officers, 1850–1861," in the Georgia Department of Archives and History in Atlanta, lists by county the sheriffs, clerks of courts, tax receivers, tax collectors, coroners, county surveyors, and ordinaries for the period. "Justices of the Inferior Court, 1813–1861," another manuscript in the same department, lists by county these important officers for the period; and the names (by county) of justices of the peace may be found in the manuscript "Commissions, Justices of the Peace, 1853–1861." The Georgia Department of Archives and History furnished microfilm copies of these sources for the author. The typewritten copy of the "Roster of State and County Officers Commissioned by the Governor of Florida, 1845–1868" and the typewritten copy "List of Legislative Members" in the Florida State Library, Tallahassee, Florida, give names of state and county officials of that state. The manuscript "Civil Register of County Officials, 1848–1867," vol. III, in the Alabama State Department of Archives and History, Montgomery, names sheriffs, probate judges, and justices of the peace for Alabama, but unfortunately it does not name county commissioners. The manuscript "Register of Commissions, State of Mississippi, 1853–1857, 1858–1864" is the most complete roster of county officers found by this writer. It lists, by county, sheriffs, probate judges, circuit court clerks, probate court clerks, treasurers, assessors, surveyors, rangers, coroners, police court members, justices of the peace, constables, and some mayors. The original of this register is in the Mississippi Department of History and Archives, Jackson; the author used microfilm copies furnished by the department. A. W. Bell, *The State Register: Comprising an Historical and*

*Statistical Account of Louisiana* (Baton Rouge, 1855), names sheriffs, recorders, assessors, coroners, and justices of the peace for all parishes in 1855 but fails to list police jury members. Names of police jurors for some twenty parishes may be found in manuscript copies of police jury minutes in the Department of Archives, Louisiana State University. For Texas see the manuscripts, "Register State, County Officers, 1846 to 1854" and "Election Register, 1854–1861," in the Texas State Archives, Austin. These give state and county officers for the period and along with Tommy Yett (comp.), *Members of the Legislature of the State of Texas from 1846 to 1939* (Austin, 1939), provide a rather complete picture of those participating in governmental affairs in the antebellum period.

## *Biographical and Personal Data*

The main sources of information for personal characteristics of the individuals involved in state and county government are the manuscript returns of Schedule No. 1, Free Inhabitants, and No. 2, Slave Inhabitants, of the Seventh and Eighth Censuses of the United States, 1850 and 1860. The first of these schedules lists by family groups all free inhabitants within a county, giving their name, sex, color, age, occupation, property owned, and place of birth by state or country. In Schedule No. 2, Slave Inhabitants, slaves within the county are listed by holders. The originals of these returns, estimated by the author to number at least 120,000 pages for the seven states of the lower South, are in the National Archives, Washington, D.C.; the writer used microfilm copies (109 rolls) in the Library of the University of Texas, Austin, and the Library of Lamar State College of Technology, Beaumont, Texas. Descriptions of these returns and their value in historical research may be found in Barnes F. Lathrop, "History from the Census Returns," *Southwestern Historical Quarterly,* LI (April, 1948), 293–312, and in Frank L. and Harriet C. Owsley, "The Economic Basis of Society in the Late Ante-Bellum South," *Journal of Southern History,* VI (February, 1940), 24–25. For a description of some of the limitations in the use of these returns, see Appendix A to Sam B. Warner, Jr., *Streetcar Suburbs* (Cambridge, Mass., 1962), 169–78.

Biographical data gathered from the manuscript census materials have been supplemented by information obtained from the *Biographical Directory of the American Congress, 1774–1961* (Washington, 1961); Allen Johnson, *et al.* (eds.), *Dictionary of American Biography* (22 vols. and index; New York, 1958); Charles R. Lee, *The Confederate Constitutions* (Chapel Hill, 1963); J. C. Hemphill (ed.), *Men of Mark in South Carolina* (4 vols.; Washington, 1907); Emily Bellinger Reynolds and Joan Reynolds Faunt (comps.), *Biographical Directory of the Senate of South Carolina, 1776–1964* (Columbia, 1964); John Amasa May and Joan Reynolds Faunt, *South Carolina Secedes* (Columbia, 1960); John B. O'Neall, *Biographical Sketches of the Bench and Bar of South Carolina* (2 vols.; Charleston, 1859); George White, *Statistics of the State of Georgia* (Savannah, 1849); Stephen F. Miller, *The Bench and Bar of Georgia* (2 vols.; Philadelphia, 1858); Ruth Blair (comp.), *Georgia's Official Register, 1925* (Atlanta, 1925); Thomas A. Owen, *History of Alabama and Dictionary of Alabama Biography* (4 vols.; Chicago, 1921); Willis Brewer, *Alabama: Her History, Resources, War Record and Public Men* (Montgomery, 1872); James D. Lynch, *The Bench and Bar of Mississippi* (New York, 1881); Dunbar Rowland, *The Official and Statistical Register of the State of Mississippi* (Madison.

Wis., 1917), and *Courts, Judges, and Lawyers of Mississippi, 1798–1935* (Jackson, 1935); Henry Foote, *Bench and Bar of the South and the Southwest* (St. Louis, 1876), and *Casket of Reminiscences* (Washington, 1874); Mary L. McLure, *Louisiana Leaders, 1830–1860* (Shreveport, 1935); Dave H. Brown (comp.), *A History of Who's Who in Louisiana Politics in 1916* (New Orleans, 1916); Joseph K. Menn, "The Great Slaveholders of Louisiana" (M.A. thesis, University of Texas, 1961); Walter P. Webb (ed.), *The Handbook of Texas* (2 vols.; Austin, 1952); *Biographical Directory of the Texan Conventions and Congresses, 1832–1845* (Huntsville, 1942); L. E. Daniell, *Personnel of the Texas State Government with Sketches of Representative Men of Texas* (San Antonio, 1892); J. H. Davenport, *The History of the Supreme Court of the State of Texas* (Austin, 1917); James D. Lynch, *The Bench and Bar of Texas* (St. Louis, 1885); and James T. DeShields, *They Sat in High Places* (San Antonio, 1940).

The published papers and memoirs of contemporaries supplement the documentary and biographical materials noted above. Particularly informative for South Carolina are "The Memoirs of Frederick Adolphus Porcher," edited by Samuel Gaillard Stoney, in the *South Carolina Historical and Genealogical Magazine,* XLVII (April, 1946), 83–108, and Benjamin F. Perry, *Reminiscences of Public Men* (Philadelphia, 1883). Rowland H. Rerick, *Memoirs of Florida* (2 vols.; Atlanta, 1902), adds information for that state as does Reuben Davis, *Recollections of Mississippi and Mississippians* (Boston, 1891), for Mississippi. Superior to both, however, is William Garrett, *Reminiscences of Public Men in Alabama for Thirty Years* (Atlanta, 1872). Garrett was for years secretary of state of Alabama, and his work contains sketches of the legislature and personalities in Alabama government from 1837 to the Civil War. Also his memoirs include valuable rosters of members of the legislature, courts, and executive offices for Alabama. Less valuable for Texas are *Rip Ford's Texas* (Austin, 1963), the edited memoirs of a prominent Texan of the nineteenth century, and Francis R. Lubbock's *Six Decades in Texas* (Austin, 1900), the memoirs of Texas' Civil War governor.

Contemporary newspapers contain news items on legislative happenings, election contests, and often on matters of local governmental concern. Too, they are the best sources of information for the political affiliation of legislators. Among the many newspapers consulted, the writer found particularly useful for this study the Augusta (Ga.) *Chronicle and Sentinel,* Charleston *Daily Courier,* Columbus (Ga.) *Enquirer,* Galveston *Weekly News,* New Orleans *Daily Delta,* New Orleans *Daily Crescent,* New Orleans *Bee,* New Orleans *Picayune,* San Antonio *Herald,* Vicksburg *Whig,* and the *Texas State Gazette.*

## *The Antebellum Period*

No student of the antebellum period can ignore the splendid *History of the South* series, published by the Louisiana State University Press and the Littlefield Fund for Southern History of the University of Texas. The two volumes of the series which relate to this period are Charles S. Sydnor, *The Development of Southern Sectionalism, 1819–1848* (Baton Rouge, 1948), and Avery O. Craven, *The Growth of Southern Nationalism, 1848–1861* (Baton Rouge, 1953). While both are thorough studies by two of the nation's outstanding scholars, the Sydnor volume is more valuable here because of its two excellent chapters summarizing state and county governmental developments in the early nineteenth century. These volumes should be supplemented by Fletcher M. Green's *Constitutional Development in the South Atlantic States, 1776–1860* (Chapel Hill, 1930), a pioneer study in southern constitutional history by a recognized authority, and two articles by the same author, "Democracy in the Old South," *Journal of Southern History,* XII (February, 1946), 3–23, and "Cycles of American Democracy," *Mississippi Valley Historical Review,* XLVIII (June, 1961), 3–23. Along with a recent study by Chilton Williamson, *American Suffrage: From Property to Democracy, 1760–1860* (Princeton, 1960), these works constitute an invaluable guide to the study of governmental developments in pre-Civil War America.

## *Constitutional Developments*

Constitutional developments in several states have been traced in monographs and unpublished theses. Among these are Ethel K. Ware, *A Constitutional History of Georgia* (New York, 1947); Albert Berry Saye, *A Constitutional History of Georgia, 1732–1945* (Athens, 1948); Malcolm Cook McMillan, *Constitutional Development in Alabama, 1798–1901: A Study in Politics, the Negro, and Sectionalism* (Chapel Hill, 1955); Winbourne Magruder Drake, "Constitutional Development in Mississippi, 1817–1865" (Ph.D. dissertation, University of North Carolina, 1954); Jean Garrett, "Amendments and Proposed Amendments to the Constitution of 1798" (M.A. thesis, University of Georgia, 1944); and James W. Prothro, "A Study of Constitutional Developments in the Office of Governor of Louisiana" (M.A. thesis, Louisiana State University, 1948).

Studies of specific constitutions are James B. Whitfield, "Florida's First Constitution," *Florida Historical Quarterly,* XVII (October, 1938), 73–83; F. W. Hoskins, "The St. Joseph

Convention," *Florida Historical Quarterly,* XVI (July–October, 1937), 33–43, 95–109; Malcolm Cook McMillan, "The Alabama Constitution of 1819: A Study of Constitution-Making on the Frontier," *Alabama Review,* III (October, 1950), 263–85; Winbourne Magruder Drake, "The Mississippi Constitutional Convention of 1832," *Journal of Southern History,* XXIII (August, 1957), 354–70; Frederic L. Paxson, "The Constitution of Texas, 1845," *Southwestern Historical Quarterly,* XVIII (April, 1915), 386–98; and Annie Laura Middleton, "The Formation of the Texas Constitution of 1845" (M.A. thesis, University of Texas, 1920).

### *Legislative Representation*

Several studies deal with the complicated subject of legislative apportionment and representation. Among these, two older studies, Chauncey S. Boucher, "Sectionalism, Representation, and the Electoral Question in Ante-Bellum South Carolina," *Washington University Studies,* vol. IV (October, 1916), and William A. Schaper, "Sectionalism and Representation in South Carolina," American Historical Association *Annual Report,* 1900, vol. I (Washington, 1901), are still standard works for South Carolina. Articles by Lucien E. Roberts, "Sectional Factors in the Movements for Legislative Reapportionment and Reduction in Georgia, 1777–1860," in *Studies in Georgia History and Government* (Athens, 1940), 94–122, and James C. Bonner, "Legislative Apportionment and County Voting in Georgia since 1777," in *Georgia Historical Quarterly,* XLVII (December, 1963), 351–73, add much light to the Georgia story. An excellent article by Roger W. Shugg, "Suffrage and Representation in Ante-Bellum Louisiana," *Louisiana Historical Quarterly,* XIX (April, 1936), 390–406, and a thorough study by Emmett Asseff, *Apportionment in Louisiana* (Baton Rouge, 1950), cover this subject for Louisiana.

Aspects of state administration are covered in Robert B. Highsaw and Carl D. Milligan, Jr., *The Growth of State Administration in Mississippi* (University, Miss., 1950), and Melvin Evans, *A Study in State Government of Louisiana* (Baton Rouge, 1932). An M.A. thesis by Ben B. Taylor, Jr., "The Appointive and Removal Powers of the Governor of Louisiana" (Louisiana State University, 1935), surveys this subject in a state where the governor's powers were reduced in the second quarter of the nineteenth century. A recent study by Fred Gantt, Jr., *The Chief Executive in Texas* (Austin, 1964), emphasizes post-Civil War governors but contains some information on the early evolution of the executive office in Texas.

## *State Administration and Courts*

Several articles deal with state courts and, along with works listed earlier under biographical data, provide an outline of southern judicial history. Among these, articles by Bond Almand in the *Georgia Bar Journal,* "The Supreme Court of Georgia: An Account of Its Delayed Birth," VI (November, 1943), 95–110, and "History of the Supreme Court of Georgia —the First Hundred Years: Part one—January 1, 1846, to June 30, 1858," VI (February, 1944), 177–206, are extremely valuable. Charles J. Hilkey, "History of the Supreme Court of Georgia: Part two—July 1, 1858, to December 31, 1870," *Georgia Bar Journal,* VI (May, 1944), 269–307, carries the story of the Georgia judiciary on through the war. Charles D. Farris, "The Courts of Territorial Florida," *Florida Historical Quarterly,* XIX (April, 1941), 346–67, covers the early development of the judiciary in that state, as does John C. Anderson, "The

Supreme Court of Alabama, Its Organization and Sketches of Chief Justices," *Alabama Historical Quarterly,* II (Spring, 1940), 23–27, for Alabama. William K. Dart, "The Justices of the Supreme Court," *Louisiana Historical Quarterly,* IV (January, 1921), 113–24, provides information on the early high court judges in Louisiana. For Texas see John C. Townes, "Development of the Texas Judicial System," *Quarterly of the Texas State Historical Association,* II (July, 1898), 29–53, 134–51, and Leila Clark Wynn, "A History of the Civil Courts in Texas," *Southwestern Historical Quarterly,* LX (July, 1956), 1–22.

### *County Government*

County government for the antebellum period has attracted comparatively little attention from historians and political scientists, but a few good studies dealing with this subject are available. Columbus Andrews, *Administrative County Government in South Carolina* (Chapel Hill, 1933), traces the evolution of county organization in the Palmetto state, and Melvin Clyde Hughes, *County Government in Georgia* (Athens, 1944), does the same for Georgia. Especially valuable in Hughes's study is his excellent treatment of the inferior court, the most powerful county agency ever created in that state. An M.A. thesis by Earl J. Hamilton, "County Government in Mississippi" (University of Texas, 1924), deals with the development of county units and various sub-divisions but otherwise contains little on the historical development of county government in Mississippi. Robert Dabney Calhoun, "The Origin and Early Development of County-Parish Government in Louisiana," *Louisiana Historical Quarterly,* XVIII (January, 1935), 56–160, is a lengthy study of the growth of county-parish government in Louisiana and provides a sound analysis of the evolution of the police jury. There are several studies of Texas local government. An article by Seymour Connor, "The Evolution of County Government in the Republic of Texas," *Southwestern Historical Quarterly,* LV (October, 1951), 163–200, and two University of Texas bulletins, Herman G. James, *County Government in Texas* (rev. ed. by Irvin Stewart; Austin, 1925), and Wallace C. Murphy, *County Government and Administration in Texas* (Austin, 1933), trace the development of Texas county government; but these should be supplemented by two superior works, V. O. Key, "A History of Texas County Government" (M.A. thesis, University of Texas, 1930), and Dick Smith, "The Development of Local Government Units in Texas" (Ph.D. dissertation, Harvard University, 1938).

## *Political Parties*

There have been numerous studies of political parties in the various southern states. A. C. Cole's *Whig Party in the South* (1914; reprint, Gloucester, Mass., 1962) was a pioneer treatise on one of the two major parties in the antebellum South. In recent years Cole's thesis that the Whigs were a class party has been re-examined in a number of works, especially the thought-provoking articles by Charles G. Sellers, Jr., "Who Were the Southern Whigs?" *American Historical Review,* LIX (January, 1954), 334–46; Grady McWhiney, "Were the Whigs a Class Party in Alabama?" *Journal of Southern History,* XXIII (November, 1957), 510–22; and by Thomas B. Alexander, *et al.,* "Who Were the Alabama Whigs?" *Alabama Review,* XVI (January, 1963), 5–19, and "The Basis of Alabama's Ante-Bellum Two-Party System," *ibid.,* XIX (October, 1966), 243–76. Paul Murray's *The Whig Party in Georgia, 1825–1853* (Chapel Hill, 1948) is a thorough examination of that party in a key southern state. Two Ph.D. dissertations at Louisiana State University, one by Leslie M. Norton, "A History of the Whig Party in Louisiana" (1940), and the other by William H. Adams, III, "The Louisiana Whig Party" (1960), describe the Whigs in that state. One of the finest political studies available is that by Herbert J. Doherty, Jr., *The Whigs of Florida, 1845–1854* (*University of Florida Monographs, Social Sciences,* No. 1, Winter, 1959; Gainesville, 1959). A recent Ph.D. dissertation at the University of Georgia (1962) by Carlton L. Jackson, "A History of the Whig Party in Alabama, 1828–1860," describes the activities of the Whig party in Alabama. Thomas B. Alexander in "Persistent Whiggery in Alabama and the Lower South, 1860–1867," *Alabama Review,* XII (January, 1959), 35–52, and in "Persistent Whiggery in the Confederate South, 1860–1877," *Journal of Southern History,* XXVII (August, 1961), 305–29, examines the continuation of Whig ideas in the postwar South.

W. Darrell Overdyke's *The Know-Nothing Party in the South* (Baton Rouge, 1951) is the standard work on that movement in the South. It is supplemented by various state studies, some of which disagree with Overdyke's treatment. Among these, see Arthur W. Thompson, "Political Nativism in Florida, 1848–1860: A Phase of Anti-Secessionism," *Journal of Southern History,* XV (February, 1949), 39–65; Overdyke's own "History of the American Party in Louisiana," *Louisiana Historical Quarterly*, XV (October, 1932), 581–88, and XVI (January-October, 1933), 84–91, 256–77, 409–26, 608–27; Edith Chalin Follett, "The History of the Know Nothing Party in Louisiana" (M.A. thesis, Tulane University, 1910); Robert C. Reinders, "The Louisiana American Party and the Catholic Church," *Mid-America,* new series, XXIX (October, 1958),

218–28; Leon Cyprian Soulé, *The Know Nothing Party in New Orleans: A Reappraisal* (Baton Rouge, 1961); Litha Crews, "The Know Nothing Party in Texas" (M.A. thesis, University of Texas, 1925); Frank H. Smyrl, "Unionism in Texas, 1856–1861," *Southwestern Historical Quarterly,* LXVIII (October, 1964), 172–95; and Sister Paul of the Cross McGrath, *Political Nativism in Texas, 1825–1860* (Washington, 1930). These should be supplemented by a recent thoughtful essay by James H. Broussard, "Some Determinants of Know-Nothing Electoral Strength in the South, 1856," in the *Journal of the Louisiana Historical Association,* VII (Winter, 1966), 5–20.

While many general political histories treat the Democratic party, few works have been written specifically on that subject. For exceptions see William T. Cash, *History of the Democratic Party in Florida* (Tallahassee, 1936); Arthur W. Thompson, *Jacksonian Democracy on the Florida Frontier* (*University of Florida Monographs, Social Sciences,* Winter, 1961; Gainesville, 1961); Edwin A. Miles, *Jacksonian Democracy in Mississippi* (*James Sprunt Studies in History and Political Science;* Chapel Hill, 1960); and Frank C. Adams (ed.), *Texas Democracy, a Centennial History of Politics and Personalities of the Democratic Party, 1836–1936* (4 vols.; Austin, 1937), especially vol. I.

## *Political Developments*

There is an abundance of studies dealing with political developments in individual states. Harold S. Schultz, *Nationalism and Sectionalism in South Carolina, 1852–1860* (Durham, 1950), adequately traces the struggle for supremacy in state affairs between the wings of the Democratic party. Two older works, U. B. Phillips, "Georgia and State Rights," American

Historical Association *Annual Report,* 1901, vol. II (Washington, 1902), and Richard Shryock, *Georgia and the Union in 1850* (Durham, 1926), are still among the finest for the antebellum period. These should be supplemented by Horace Montgomery's excellent *Cracker Parties* (Baton Rouge, 1950) and two articles by Paul Murray, "The Crisis of 1850 and Its Effects on Political Parties in Georgia" and "Party Organization in Georgia Politics, 1825–1853," in *Georgia Historical Quarterly,* XXIV (December, 1940), 293–322, and XXIX (December, 1945), 195–210. A doctoral dissertation by Edwin Lacy Williams, Jr., "Florida in the Union, 1845–1861" (University of North Carolina, 1951), covers the political and constitutional history of Florida as a state. There are a series of volumes covering Alabama politics for the pre-Civil War period. Particularly valuable for this study is Lewy Dorman's *Party Politics in Alabama from 1850 through 1860* (Wetumpka, Alabama, 1935). Not only does Dorman cover political developments, but he also has an important appendix listing legislative members with party affiliation for the period. In addition to the Miles work mentioned earlier, Donald M. Rawson, "Party Politics in Mississippi, 1850–1860" (Ph.D. dissertation, Vanderbilt University, 1964), and Percy Lee Rainwater, *Mississippi: Storm Center of Secession, 1856–1861* (Baton Rouge, 1938), furnish much material on political developments within the state. Several studies cover Louisiana politics for the period. James K. Greer's *Louisiana Politics, 1845–1861* (Baton Rouge, 1930) is a thorough narrative and contains much information on gubernatorial and legislative contests. Roger W. Shugg's *Origins of Class Struggle in Louisiana* (Baton Rouge, 1939) covers a much broader sweep of time and is highly interpretative, but contains a sound analysis of constitutional and political developments. Perry H. Howard's *Political Tendencies in Louisiana, 1812–1952* (Baton Rouge, 1957) is useful but heavily emphasizes presidential and gubernatorial elections and is less valuable for the present study than the works by Greer and Shugg. Regrettably, little has been written on Texas political developments for the period, but Ernest W. Winkler's *Platforms of Political Parties in Texas* (Austin, 1916) contains not only platforms but also a short history of party organization for the antebellum period. And Earl W. Fornell, *The Galveston Era* (Austin, 1961), ably discusses political developments in Texas' largest city on the eve of the Civil War.

### *Supplemental Information*

Much information on state government may be found in biographies of key political figures of the period. Lillian A. Kibler's *Benjamin F. Perry, South Carolina Unionist* (Durham, 1946), for example, traces Perry's fight for reform in legislative apportionment and elections in conservative South Carolina. Elizabeth Merritt, *James Henry Hammond, 1807–1864* (Baltimore, 1923), and Robert C. Tucker, "James Henry Hammond, South Carolinian" (Ph.D. dissertation, University of North Carolina, 1958), cover the career of a powerful figure who influenced both state and national politics. There are biographies of a number of prominent Georgians, but they deal largely with their role on the national rather than the state scene. Daisy Parker, "John Milton, Governor of Florida," *Florida Historical Quarterly,* XX (April, 1942), 348–61, traces the career of Florida's last antebellum governor. An M.A. thesis by Virginia Estella Knapp, "William Phineas Browne, A Yankee Business Man of the South" (University of Texas, 1948), is particularly informative on Alabama state affairs in the 1840's. Browne, who was first a Whig and later a Democrat, served in the Alabama house of representatives in the mid-forties and described various members of the Alabama legislature for the period. Two Ph.D. dissertations, one by James H. McLendon, "John Quitman" (University of Texas, 1949) and the other by John Edmond Gonzales, "The Public Career of Henry Stuart Foote, 1804–1880" (University of North Carolina, 1957), describe the activities of two of the South's most colorful governors. A series of M.A. theses written at Louisiana State University and later published in the *Louisiana Historical Quarterly* includes Sidney J. Aucoin, "The Political Career of Isaac Johnson, Governor of Louisiana, 1846–1850," XXVIII (July, 1945), 941–89; Albert Leonce Dupont, "The Political Career of Paul Octave Hébert, Governor of Louisiana, 1853–1856," XXXI (April, 1948), 491–552; Thomas R. Landry, "The Political Career of Robert Charles Wickliffe, Governor of Louisiana, 1856–1860," XXV (July, 1942), 640–727; and Van D. Odom, "The Political Career of Thomas Overton Moore, Secession Governor of Louisiana," XXVI (October, 1943), 975–1054. For Governor Moore, see also G. P. Whittington, "Thomas O. Moore, Governor of Louisiana," *Louisiana Historical Quarterly,* XIII (January, 1930), 3–31. For Texas, various biographies of Sam Houston, especially *Sam Houston: The Great Designer* (Austin, 1954) by Llerena Friend, contain much relating to state politics. Little has been done on Texas' other pre-Civil War governors, but helpful studies are Benjamin H. Miller, "Elisha Marshall Pease, A Biography" (M.A. thesis, University of Texas, 1927); Elizabeth Yates Morris, "James Pinckney Henderson" (M.A. thesis, University of Texas, 1931); and S. H. German, "Governor George Thomas Wood," *Southwestern Historical Quarterly,* XX (January, 1917), 260–68.

# INDEX

Acadians, 59
Adams County, Miss.: board of police, 86–87
Adams, James Hopkins, 55n
Adjutant general: how chosen in Georgia, 26
Africans, 25
Age requirements: in Georgia, 13; in Florida, 14; in Louisiana, 19
Ages: of county officers, 95; of governors, 52, 56–60; of justices, 157; of legislators, 28–29, 32, 49, 110, 121, 126, 129, 134, 139, 144
Alabama: 21; American party in, 112; apportionment in, 108; black belt, 4; chancery court, 74; commissioners court of revenue and roads, 83, 90, 115; comptroller of public accounts, 48, 63; Constitution of 1819, pp. 20, 48, 73, 90; constitutional amendments, 20–21, 73–74; county officers, 90; democratic reform in, 20, 107; Democrats, 45; Federal Ratio, 20; governor of, 48, 53, 58–59, 61, 113; judges, 73–74, 79, 108, 114; justices of the peace, 67, 93; legislature, 20–21, 29, 30–31, 35, 37–39, 40–41, 45, 73, 91, 111, 114, 121–25; militia officers, 48; population of, 4n; probate judge, 68; property qualifications, 20–21, 107; residency requirements of, 53; secretary of state, 48, 63; senators, 37; sheriffs, 95–96; suffrage, 21; supreme court of, 73, 78; treasurer, 48, 63; Whigs, 43–46
Allen, J. Duncan, 34
Allston, Robert F. W., 55n
American Party, 43n, 47, 112
Appeals courts, 70–71
Apportionment: in Alabama, 107–108; in Florida, 108; in Georgia, 108; in Louisiana, 17–18, 116; in Texas, 24
Ascension Parish, La., 88
Attorney general, 19, 50, 61–63
Auditor of public accounts: in Mississippi, 22, 62
Autauga County, Ala., 67

Banking, 25, 27
Bank presidents: barred from holding office, 15, 54, 110
Barbour County, Ala., 67
Baylor, R. E. B., 79
Bell, Peter H., 60
Benjamin, Judah P., 19
Benning, Henry L., 78
Bibb, Thomas, 58
Bibb, William W., 58
Birthplaces: of county officers, 96; of Georgia justices, 44; of legislators, 122, 126, 130, 135, 140, 145, 150

Black belt, 17
Black counties, 46, 101, 104–105
Black parishes, 19, 34
Blacksmiths: in county government, 98; on Georgia Inferior Court, 158
Board of commissioners (Fla.): 14, 83, 92, 98; ages of, 95; birthplaces of, 96; how chosen, 92; occupations of, 97–98; powers of, 115; property holding of, 99–102; slaveholding of, 103–104, 160
Board of police (Miss.): 83, 86; in Adams County, 86–87; ages of, 95; birthplaces of, 96; in black counties, 104–105; occupations of, 97–98; powers of, 115; property holding of, 99–101, 162; rotation on, 93; slaveholding of, 102–104, 162
Board of public works (La.), 62
Brandon, Gerald C., 57
Brazoria County, Tex., 102
Brazos River, 102
Brickmasons: in county government, 98
Briscoe, Waters, 94
Broome, James E., 60
Brown, Albert Gallatin, 57
Brown, Joseph E., 12, 56, 56n
Brown, Thomas, 60, 113

Cairnes, Joseph, 102
Calhoun, John C., 3, 5
Carpenters: in county government, 98
Chambers County, Ala., 67
Chancery court, 74
Chapman, Reuben, 59
Charleston, S. C., 7, 81–82
Chief justices (Tex.), 69, 76, 97
Chilton, William P., 78
Circuit courts: 68, 70, 114; in Alabama, 74; in Mississippi, 77; in South Carolina, 64–65
Citizenship, 52–53
Civil cases, 75
Clark, Charles, 32
Clay, Clement, 58
Cobb, Howell: 9; as governor of Georgia, 56, 56n
Collier, Henry W., 59
Colorado River, 102
Commissioner of land office (Tex.), 62–63
Commissioners court of revenue and roads (Ala.), 83, 90, 115
Commissioners for the poor (S. C.), 92, 115
Commissioners of roads and bridges (S. C.): 83, 88; ages of, 95; how chosen, 115; occupations of, 97; property holding of, 98–99, 100–101; slaveholding of, 103–104
Commissioners of treasury (S. C.), 7
Commission on Vacant Offices, 88
Compromise of 1808, p. 7
Compromise of 1850, p. 9
Comptroller: in Alabama, 48, 63; in Texas, 62
Constable, 82, 86, 89, 90–92, 115
Constitution of 1789 (Ga.), 12
Constitution of 1790 (S. C.), 6, 52
Constitution of 1798 (Ga.), 10, 12, 26, 66, 71, 94
Constitution of 1812 (La.), 15, 16, 50–53, 75

Constitution of 1817 (Miss.), 22, 90
Constitution of 1819 (Ala.), 20, 48, 73, 90
Constitution of 1832 (Miss.), 22, 53–54, 61, 77, 91
Constitution of 1836 (Tex.), 24, 76
Constitution of 1838 (Fla.), 14, 52, 74
Constitution of 1845 (La.), 17, 18, 24, 51–53, 75–76, 96
Constitution of 1852 (La.), 19, 51–53, 75, 91, 108
Constitutional amendments: in Alabama, 20–21, 73–74; in Florida, 75; in Georgia, 13, 24, 26, 53, 72, 90; in Mississippi, 77; in Texas, 24, 76
Constitutional conventions: in Georgia, 11; in Louisiana, 17, 19; in Mississippi, 22, 58, 77
Coroner, 82, 89, 90, 91, 92, 115
Corporations, 27
County boards, 99, 102–104
County clerk, 89, 90, 92, 93, 115
County commissioners: in Texas, 93, 98
County court: 83, 84, 115; in Georgia, 84; in Mississippi, 83, 90, 91; in South Carolina, 64–65; in Texas, 83–84, 93, 95–97, 99, 100–101, 103–104, 115, 163
County judge, 68–69, 70n, 91
County officers: 95, 115; in Alabama, 90; birthplaces of, 96; duties of, 89; in Florida, 92; in Georgia, 90, 96; in Mississippi, 87, 90–91; occupations of, 97–98; property holding of, 100–101; property requirements for, 98–99; rotation of, 92–93, 105, 117; in South Carolina, 92, 94, 115; in Texas, 92
Court clerk, 50–51, 92
Court of chancery (Miss.), 77
Court of errors (S. C.), 70–71
Court of the ordinary (Ga.), 66
Court of probate (Miss.), 68
Craftsmen: in legislatures, 33
Crayonmaker: in county government, 98
Criminal cases, 75

Dargan, Edmund, 78
Declaration of Rights (Miss.), 22–23
Democratic reform: 105; in Alabama, 20; in Mississippi, 20; in Texas, 23–24
Democrats: 43–47, 112; in Alabama, 59, 126; in Georgia, 134; in Florida, 60; in Louisiana, 59, 138; in Mississippi, 58, 143
District attorney: in Louisiana, 51
District courts, 114
District judges: in Louisiana, 75; in Texas, 79
Donaldson, Joseph, 94
Drake, Winbourne Magruder, 76–77
Dueling, 54
Duelists: barred from office, 15, 25, 54, 110

Eggleston, E. C., 102
Engineers, 98
Equity, 70, 77, 114
Executive officers, 19, 26, 62–63

Factor, 98
Farmers: as county officers, 97, 158; in legislatures, 27, 33, 40, 110, 123, 127, 131, 136, 141, 146, 151
Federal Ratio: in Alabama, 20, 108; in Florida, 14; in Georgia, 10
Florida: 9; apportionment in, 108; board of commissioners, 14, 83, 92, 95, 96, 97–98, 99–104, 115, 160; constitution of, 13, 14, 52, 74–75; counties, 82; county officers, 69, 92; democratic reform in, 107; governor of, 13, 49, 52–54, 60–61, 113; judges, 14, 69, 74, 114; justices of the peace, 67; legislature, 13–14, 26, 29, 30, 35, 39–42, 45, 126–28; population of, 4n; residency requirement of, 14–15; suffrage, 13; Whigs, 43, 45, 46
Franklin Parish, La.: expenditures, 88

Garrett, William, 63n
Georgia: 9, 82; American party in, 112; apportionment in, 108; constitution of, 10, 12, 13, 26, 66, 71, 72, 90, 94; conventions, 11; counties, 82, 84, 90, 96; democratic reform in, 107; governor of, 26, 49, 52, 53, 56, 61, 66, 113; inferior courts of, 65–67, 72, 83, 90, 94–101, 103–104, 115, 157–59; judges, 26, 64, 72; justices of the peace, 64, 65, 67, 72; legislature, 10, 13, 28–31, 35–41, 45, 49, 90, 94, 108, 111, 114, 129–34; militia, 26; population of, 4n; secretary of state, 26; suffrage, 12–13; supreme court of, 71, 78; surveyor general of, 26; Whigs, 43, 45–46
Gibbons, Lyman, 78
Gist, William H., 55n
Governors: ages of, 52, 57; in Alabama, 48, 58–59, 61, 113; in Florida, 49, 60–61, 113; in Georgia, 26, 49, 56, 61, 66, 113; in Louisiana, 50, 52, 59–62, 75, 90, 113; in Mississippi, 49, 57–58, 113; occupations of, 54–60; party affiliations of, 54–60; personal characteristics of, 54–60; powers of, 25, 113–14; property requirement for, 53; residency requirement for, 52, 113; in South Carolina, 49, 52, 55, 109, 113; in Texas, 49, 60, 62, 76
Grimball, John A., 62
Grimes, Jesse, 32
Guion, John I., 57–58
Gulf states: county officers, 96

Habersham County, Ga., 66
Hancock, John, 79
Hébert, Paul Octave, 59
Hemphill, John, 79n, 80
High Court of Errors and Appeals, 22, 77
Hill, L. M., 37
Holmes County, Fla., 102
Holmes, David, 57
Hotelkeepers, 158
Houston, Sam: governor of Texas, 60; influence in state, 111

Immigrants: in New Orleans, 17
Independents, 112

Indians, 25
Inferior court (Ga.): 65–67, 83, 90; ages of members, 95, 157; birthplaces of members, 96, 157; how chosen, 72; occupations of members, 97–98, 158; powers of, 115; property holding of members, 98–101, 158–59; rotation, 94; slaveholding of members, 103–104, 159

Jackson County, Ala., 67
Jacksonian Democracy: 5, 94; effects of, 9, 22, 73, 92
Jailer, 86
Johnson, Herschel V., 9, 56
Johnson, Isaac, 59
Judges: 64, 78–79, 114; in Alabama, 73, 114; in Florida, 114; in Georgia, 26, 72, 108, 114; in Louisiana, 19, 50, 114; in Mississippi, 114; in South Carolina, 7, 64–65, 114; in Texas, 24, 114
Judiciary, 64, 114
Justices of the peace: 64, 67, 72, 82, 89, 90–92, 105, 114–15; in Alabama, 67, 90, 93; in Florida, 67, 92; in Georgia, 64–65, 67, 72, 90; in Louisiana, 51, 90–91; in Mississippi, 90–91; in South Carolina, 64, 92; in Texas, 67, 98

Kentucky, 96
Know Nothing party, 43n, 47, 112

Laborers: in county government, 98; in legislatures, 33
Lawyers: in county government, 97, 158; as governors, 54, 57–59; in legislatures, 27, 33, 45, 110, 123, 127, 131, 136, 141, 146, 151
Leake, Walter, 57n
Legislators: ages of, 28, 29, 32, 110, 121, 126, 129, 134, 139, 144; birthplaces of, 31, 32, 44, 110–11, 122, 127, 130, 135, 140, 145, 150; occupations of, 28, 33, 35, 123, 127, 131, 141, 146, 151; property holding of, 39, 40, 45, 116, 124–25, 128, 132–33, 137, 142, 147, 152; as slaveholders, 37, 38, 41, 43–44, 111, 116, 125, 128, 133–34, 138, 143, 148, 153
Legislature: in Alabama, 38–39; in Florida, 13–14, 42; in Georgia, 11–12, 38, 90, 94; in Louisiana, 39, 51, 116; in Mississippi, 23, 39; powers of, 25, 26, 27, 48–49, 50, 61, 71, 73, 91–92, 108–109, 114; representation in, 10, 11–12, 14–15, 17–18, 21; residency requirement for, 8–9, 13, 21; rotation in, 41–42, 111; in South Carolina, 6, 33, 36, 49, 94; in Texas, 24, 39, 149
Leon County, Fla., 102
Lieutenant governor, 61–62
Lipscomb, Abner S., 79n
Louisiana: 9, 112; age requirements for office holding, 19; American party in, 112; apportionment in, 17–18, 116; attorney general, 50; black belt, 17, 19; Constitution of 1812, pp. 15, 16, 50–53, 75; Constitution of 1845, pp. 17, 18, 51–53, 75, 91; Constitution of 1852, pp. 19,

51–53, 75, 91, 108; convention of 1852, p. 19; court clerks, 51; democratic advances in, 15; Democrats, 43; executive officers of, 50; governor of, 50–52, 53, 54, 59–60, 61–62, 75, 113; judges, 19, 50, 74–75, 114; justices of the peace, 51; legislature, 29, 30, 32, 35, 39, 40–41, 50–51, 110–11, 116, 134–38; lieutenant governor, 61; local government, 81; parishes, 69, 81, 87, 91; police jury, 68, 83–84, 87, 90–91, 93, 95–102, 104, 115, 161; politics, 112; population of, 4n; reapportionment in, 16; residency requirements of, 18–19; sheriff, 51, 86; suffrage, 15, 19, 108; supreme court of, 75, 79; treasurer, 50; Whig party, 43–45

Lower South: characteristics of, 4; circuit courts, 70; and Compromise of 1850, p. 9; county officers, 81–91, 95–96, 98–99, 105, 115–116; geography of, 3; governors, 48, 52, 112–13; judiciary, 78, 114; legislators, 26–27, 30–31, 44; political parties in, 42–43; suffrage, 105; Whigs, 46

Lowndes County, Miss., 102

Lumpkin, Joseph Henry, 78

McCaw, Robert G., 35, 36

McDonald, Charles J., 78

Macfarlan, Allan, 35, 36

McMillan, Malcolm Cook, 48

McWillie, William, 57

Manning, John L., 34, 37, 55, 55n

Marshall, J. F., 34

Martin, Joshua, 59

Matagorda County, Tex., 102

Means, John Hugh, 55n

Mechanics, 33, 98, 158

Merchants: in Alabama, 123; in county government, 97, 158; in Florida, 127; in Georgia, 138; in Louisiana, 19, 108, 136; in South Carolina, 146; in Texas, 151

Mexico, 24

Militia: 113; officers, 26, 48; requirements for voting, 20, 22–24, 91

Ministers: in Alabama legislature, 123; barred from office, 15, 25, 54, 110; in county government, 98, 158

Mississippi: attorney general, 62; auditor of public accounts, 62; board of police, 83, 86, 91, 93, 95–101, 103–104, 115, 162; Constitution of 1817, pp. 22, 90; Constitution of 1832, pp. 22–23, 53–54, 61, 77, 91; convention of 1817, p. 58; convention of 1832, p. 58; county officials, 68–69, 86–87, 90–91; courts, 68, 77, 83, 91; democratic reform in, 20–21, 107; Democrats, 43, 45; governor, 49, 52–53, 57–58, 113; High Court of Errors and Appeals, 22, 77; judges, 73–74, 114; legislature, 23, 27, 29, 30–32, 35, 39, 40–43, 68n–69n, 91, 109, 111, 139–43; lieutenant governor, 61; militia, 22–23; population of, 4n; representatives, 23; residency requirements of, 23; secretary of state, 62; senators,

23; slaves, 4; suffrage, 22–23, 91, 107; tax requirements of, 22–23
Missouri, 96
Montgomery Convention, 78
Moore, Andrew B., 59, 59n
Moore, Gabriel, 58
Mouton, Alexander, 59

Negroes, 86, 107
New Orleans, La., 16–18, 47n, 75, 81–82
Nisbet, Eugenius A., 78
Northern states, 32
Notaries public, 90, 136

Occupations: of Alabama legislators, 123; of county officers, 97–98, 158; of Florida legislators, 127; of Georgia legislators, 28, 131; of legislators, 27, 35; of Louisiana legislators, 136; of Mississippi legislators, 141; of South Carolina legislators, 146; of Texas legislators, 151
Ochiltree, William B., 79
Officeholding requirements, 109–10
Olmsted, Frederick Law: visits South Carolina, 5
O'Neall, John Belton, 71
Opposition party, 46, 112
Overseers: in county government, 98

Parish: government of, 87–88; officers, 69, 86, 90–91, 99; revenue, 87–88
Parkhill, George W., 102
Pease, Elisha M., 60
Pee Dee River, 3
Pendleton, Henry, 64
Personal property: of county officers, 98–101, 159, 160, 162–63; of legislators, 40, 125, 128, 133, 137, 142, 147, 152
Physicians: in county government, 97, 158; in legislatures, 27, 33, 123, 127, 131, 136, 141, 146, 151
Pickens, Francis W., 55n
Poindexter, George, 58
Pointe Coupee Parish, La., 85–86
Plain folk, 6, 105, 117
Planters: in county government, 97, 103–104, 158; as governors, 54–55, 58, 60; in legislatures, 27, 33, 36, 39, 40, 110–11, 123, 127, 131, 136, 141, 146, 151; in Louisiana, 19, 108; in South Carolina, 6
Police jury: 68, 83–84, 87; ages of members, 95; birthplaces of members, 96; how chosen, 90–91; occupations of members, 97–98; in Pointe Coupee Parish, 85–86; powers of, 84, 86, 115; property holding of members, 99–101, 161; rotation, 93; slaveholdings of members, 103–104, 161; in St. Charles Parish, 86–87; in Tensas Parish, 87
Poll tax, 17
Presidential electors, 6, 109
Probate courts, 114
Probate judges, 68–69, 92, 114–15
Property holding: of governors, 54–60; of sheriffs, 100–101
Property qualifications, 8–9, 13, 15–16, 20–21, 22–24, 105, 108
Prosecuting attorney, 50

Quitman, John A., 57

Read, John H., 37
Reagan, John H., 79
Real property holding: of county officials, 99, 158, 160–63; of legislators, 39, 45, 124, 128, 132, 137, 142, 147, 152
Representation: in Alabama, 20–21; in Florida, 13–14; in Georgia, 10–11; in Louisiana, 15–18; in South Carolina, 7
Representatives, 13, 23, 28–29, 110
Residency requirements, 8–9, 13–15, 18–19, 23, 25, 107, 110, 113
Rhett, R. Barnwell, 3
Rio Grande River, 3
Rotation in office: 117; of county officials, 67, 69, 92–95, 105; of executive officers, 62–63; Jacksonian concept of, 92; of judges, 79; of legislature, 111
Runnels, Hardin R., 60
Rusk, Thomas J., 111

Sabine Parish, La., 87–88
St. Charles Parish, La., 86–87, 102
Sargent, Winthrop, 48n
Scott, Abram M., 57n
Secretary of state: in Alabama, 48, 61, 63; in Florida, 61; in Georgia, 26, 61; in Louisiana, 19, 50–51, 61; in Mississippi, 22, 62; in South Carolina, 7; in Texas, 63
Senators, 13, 23, 28–29, 37–38, 42, 110
Sharkey, William L., 79
Sheriff, 50–51, 82–83, 86, 89–93, 95–96, 100–101, 105, 109, 114–15
Shryock, Richard, 9
Shugg, Roger, 18
Slave counties, 58. *See* black counties
Slaveholders: in county government, 102–105, 116, 159–63; as governors, 54, 60
Slave patrols, 84, 86
Slavery, 3, 27
Slaves: regulation of, 86
Slave trader, 98
Slidell, John, 112
Slidell, Thomas, 79
South Carolina: 3, 4, 42, 82, 111–12, 116; aristocratic nature of, 4; commissioners of roads and bridges, 83, 88, 97–100, 103–105; compromise of 1808, p. 7; Constitution of 1790, pp. 6, 52; controversy with federal government, 5; county government, 105, 114; county officials, 94, 96, 105; courts, 64–65, 70–71; executive officers, 7; geographic features of, 5; governor of, 49, 52–53, 55, 109, 113; judges, 7, 64–65, 114; justices of the peace, 64; legislature, 6, 26–27, 29, 30, 33, 35–36, 39, 40–41, 49, 61, 71, 88, 90, 92, 94, 114, 144–48; lieutenant governor, 61; local officials, 7, 92, 115; population of, 4n; representatives, 7, 28, 33–34, 110; senators, 28, 33–34, 110; slaves, 4; suffrage requirements of, 6, 8, 108–109; taxes, 88
Spalding, Randolph, 37
Stephens, Alexander H., 9
Stephens, Linton, 78

Suffrage, 6, 8, 12–13, 15, 19, 21–25, 91, 98, 105, 107–109
Superintendent of education, 51, 62
Supreme court, 71, 75–76, 78–79, 114
Surveyor general, 7, 26
Surveyors, 89–92, 115, 127
Sydnor, Charles, 81

Tax collector, 83, 89, 90–92, 114–15
Taxes, 88
Tax requirements, 23, 91
Teachers, 33, 98, 158
Tennessee, 83–84, 96
Tensas Parish, La., 87
Texas: 3, 4, 42, 111; American party in, 112; apportionment in, 24; attorney general, 62–63; chief justices, 69, 76, 97; commissioner of land office, 62–63; comptroller, 62; Constitution of 1836, pp. 24, 76; Constitution of 1845, pp. 24, 76; county commissioners, 93, 98; county court, 83–84, 95–97, 99–101, 103–104, 115, 163; county judge, 69, 70n; democratic reform in, 23–24, 107; governor of, 49, 53, 60, 62, 76, 113; judges, 24, 74–76, 79, 114; justices of the peace, 67, 98; legislature, 24, 29–30, 32, 35, 39–41, 109–11, 146, 149, 151–53; lieutenant governor, 61–62; militia, 24; population of, 4n; property qualifications, 24, 107; secretary of state, 63; sheriff, 97, 105; suffrage, 24–25; treasurer, 62
Toombs, Robert, 9
Townes, Robert J., 79
Towns, George W., 56
Trades people, 27
Treasurer, 19, 22, 48, 61–63, 83, 90, 92

Union party, 46
United States Supreme Court, 72
Upper South, 3, 30–31, 32–33, 68, 83, 97, 111

Veto, 48–50, 114
Virginia, 5, 81, 83–84

Walker, Richard W., 78
Ward, Joshua J., 34, 36
Warner, Hiram, 78
West Baton Rouge Parish, La., 102
Weston, Plowden, 37
Wheeler, Royal T., 79n
Whigs: 43–45, 47, 112; in Alabama, 126; in Florida, 60; in Georgia, 134; in Louisiana, 59, 138; in Mississippi, 143
Whitfield, James, 58
Wickliffe, Robert C., 59
Williams, Robert, 48n
Winston, John A., 59, 59n
Women, 107
Wood, George T., 60

Yancey, William L., 3

Zavala County, Tex., 82

*The People in Power*

has been set on the Linotype in twelve point Granjon with two-point spacing between the lines. Fourteen point Engravers Bold was selected for display. The book was designed by Jim Billingsley and composed, printed, and bound by Kingsport Press, Inc. The paper on which the book is printed is designed for an effective life of at least three hundred years.

*The University of Tennessee Press*
*Knoxville*